WHAT HAPPENED TO JOHN?

A MEMOIR OF ENDURING LOVE, MENTAL
HEALTH, AND SUICIDE

DENISE COLLINS

1

DAY ZERO

MONDAY 29TH OCTOBER 2018

THE DAY our life ended began quite unremarkably.

As usual, John and I took our dogs for a walk across a nearby meadow. Bright yellow sunlight beamed from a cloudless blue sky, illuminating an array of colours like an artist's palette. The temperature was mild; it could almost have been spring rather than autumn. Only closer inspection of the trees, with their thinning array of red and gold leaves, rather than pink and white blossom, suggested a season of endings instead of beginnings.

Breathing in the early morning air, everything in that moment was okay. Not perfect by any means, but good enough. It had been a difficult couple of weeks. Actually, it had been a difficult couple of years. But we'd had time to let the latest sad news embed and we'd talk things over later. This was a brand new day. The start of a fresh new week. Even though we faced more impending loss, I believed we would do what we always did when things were tough; we'd find a way through it, together.

We watched our smallest dog, Lil, scamper into the long grass chasing a murder of crows. With a flurry of black shiny wings and indignant squawking, one by one they took flight while she barked and snapped at them. Lil is a scruffy Chihuahua-Yorkshire Terrier mix. Although a loveable little character, she can't be described as much of a looker. We'd inherited her when my auntie Olive died a couple of years before. I'd always promised Olive I'd take care of whatever canine companion she had at the time of her passing. Lil was not the kind of dog either John nor I would have chosen but her cheeky personality won us over and stole both of our hearts.

'She'd have a shock if she actually caught one,' I said. 'They're bigger than she is.'

A flock of geese flew, in distinctive V-formation, south across the sky. Another signal winter was on its way. They honked as if shouting directions to each other. John paused to watch them.

'Look at that,' he said. I turned in the direction he was pointing. Both the sun and moon were visible. They faced each other across the sky, the pale moon to the right illuminated by the bright sun to the left.

We continued our walk, talking about nothing in particular. An upcoming trip to Prague, our kids' birthdays. The conversation meandered, as it does between people whose lives have been entwined for a long time.

Back home, we sat at the kitchen table and had coffee. Good coffee was a passion we shared. We'd had our black and chrome bean-to-cup machine almost a year. A trip to Monchique the previous October, where we'd spent lazy mornings at a café in the square, sipping espressos from tiny white china cups, inspired the purchase.

'I feel a bit chilly.' John was almost never cold. It was always me wanting to turn up the central heating. I'd usually be adorned in several layers while John, in a short sleeved t-shirt, would assure me the temperature was just fine.

It's funny – the things you remember.

John downed his coffee and prepared to leave for work. Perhaps I should suggest he go easy on the caffeine while so on edge?

I walked with him to the hallway and noticed how tired he looked. I gave him a hug.

'I've only got a couple of estimates to do,' he said, looping his rucksack over his shoulder. 'If they're small jobs, I'll do them right away. If not, I'll get them in the diary and come home.' John was a self-employed plumber and had been for over two decades.

'Okay. I've got an appointment at the opticians. After that I'm here for the rest of the day.'

He nodded. I gave him another hug. 'I love you.'

'I love you too. See you later.'

Back home after my visit to the optician, I was talking to our son Liam on the phone, extolling the virtues of the new contact lenses I was trialling, when the dogs launched into a quartet of frenzied barking. Someone was at the door.

'I'll call you back,' I yelled over the din.

In gritty TV dramas, when two uniformed police officers appear at the front door, everyone instinctively knows it is bad news.

Not me.

Holding Doug, our escape-artist Collie, back by the collar I answered the door. I have no idea why but I jumped to the conclusion the police officers had come to talk to me about the noise of the dogs. Their collective barking was so loud I couldn't hear a word being said.

'Wait a minute, I'll shut them away,' I shouted, closing the door leaving the police officers standing outside. I ushered the still-barking dogs safely into my office.

A little like Lil, Doug was not the dog I thought I'd end up with. I think the initial idea to get a Border Collie must have been inspired by watching too many episodes of *One Man and His Dog* on the BBC. And maybe by seeing Pudsey win Britain's Got Talent. At the time we, or rather *I*, decided to get a Collie, we had two retired Greyhounds. These placid, long-legged creatures spent most of their time asleep on the sofa. I thought it would be fun to get a more active dog; I fancied the idea of taking up agility.

I'd decided on a Border Collie and diligently set about the task of researching whether I should go for a dog from a working or show line. I had phone conversations with various breeders, read books, and scanned websites.

Then one day, I acted purely on impulse.

I was in my consulting room. My last client of the morning had called to rearrange her appointment and, as I frequently did, I started searching on my phone: *Border Collie puppies for sale.* A photo of a cute litter flashed up. They were at a farm only an hour's drive away. I immediately phoned John.

'What are you up to?'

'Why?'

'Fancy going to see some puppies?'

'Absolutely!'

We were in high spirits as we put the address into the sat nav. We eagerly anticipated meeting a well-cared for working dog, dutifully nursing her litter. The reality was somewhat less idyllic.

What we found were a couple of shabby barns packed full of Collie pups, clearly from a variety of different litters and of varying ages. The man who showed us around explained that, as a way of making a bit of extra money, cash-strapped farmers in Wales bred their working dogs and sold the pups to people like him. My heart sank as I surveyed the scene. I wondered what the pups had already been through during their short lives and what might become of them.

Amid all the others, one little pup caught my attention. He had the classic black and white markings. He also had ears that stuck straight up in the air and appeared way too big for his head. Sitting in the distinctive lopsided puppy sit, he was motionless and staring right at me.

I caught John's gaze and nodded towards the little pup with the big ears.

John's expression conveyed confusion. 'I thought you wanted a fluffy one?'

John was right. The big eared pup had a short wiry coat while I had envisioned a long-haired Collie strutting at my heel around the agility course. But then, I'd also said I wanted to get a pup from a reputable breeder but here we were.

Morally, we should have walked away, making clear our condemnation of the despicable trade. But the reality was this sad looking puppy with big ears had already captivated me.

'What's this wound on his back?' I asked the so-called farmer as he handed Doug to me.

He peered indifferently at the open gash on the pup's back. 'Don't know,' he shrugged. 'Maybe one of the bigger dogs attacked him. Or maybe he scraped it trying to escape under the gate.' He went to return Doug to the barn. 'There's loads more. Choose another one.'

'No, it's okay. We'll take him.'

'Really?' John looked at me incredulously. 'Are you sure?'

And that's how we ended up with Doug. It was more like picking a goldfish from a pet shop tank rather than choosing a canine companion that could feasibly be part of our lives for the next fifteen or so years.

While I drove, John cuddled our new puppy all the way home. For the first few days, Doug seemed fine. We bathed his wound, which didn't seem as bad as it had first appeared, applied ointment, and it started to scab over. Then he got really sick. The vet had no idea what was wrong, so suggested we contact the seller to ask if any of the other pups were ill.

'If he dies, I'll give you a replacement,' was the response I got when I phoned.

Doug spent days at the vets hooked up to a drip. We were told to expect the worst but he was obviously a fighter and pulled through. However, the illness, coupled with all the trauma we think he experienced so early in his life, made him a bit different. John taught him some tricks using clicker training but, on the whole, Doug was wild.

We enrolled in puppy training, but had to stop when he came down with mange – a horrible skin disease caused by mites. John and I had to bathe him in an awful smelling purple coloured solution. Doug fought us all the way.

He also had a high chase drive; great for a working sheepdog on a Welsh hillside but less useful for a pet living in a terraced house in Chelmsford, Essex.

When he got into a chase frenzy it was impossible to control him… until John discovered an unconventional recall method. I honestly can't remember how he stumbled on it, but if John sprayed an aerosol, Doug would immediately abandon the chase and race back ready to attack the offending can. We got some very funny looks at the park when John whipped out his aerosol.

As Doug matured, he developed more weird quirks but I still harboured hopes of doing agility. I was advised that *we* had to master obedience first. So, as Doug was now mange free, I searched out training classes.

Doug never displayed any of his naughty behaviours in class. He was often quite the poster boy – clever and eager to show off how fast he could pick things up. But it was a different story back at home. When answering the door, unless I was really mindful, he would fly out of the smallest gap and run amok in the road, chasing cars. As, mercifully, he was never actually hit by one, he considered himself quite successful at rounding them up. Which encouraged him further.

At the end of one training class, I cornered the teacher. 'I got a Collie because I thought they were easy to train.'

The trainer glared at me, 'Collies *are* easy to train.' He looked down at Doug, offering him a sympathetic smile. 'You just can't train one to be a Labrador!'

One time, when Doug was being especially badly behaved, Liam asked, with more than a hint of disapproval in his voice, 'Why did you get a Collie?'

'Because they're clever,' I replied defensively.

'You could have got a Golden Retriever. They're used as guide dogs. You can't get much cleverer than that!' He had a point.

One of Doug's foibles is his dislike of anything that can take photos. Cameras, obviously, but he also somehow understands that phones are capable of taking his picture. The moment I try to take a photo with any device, his eyes widen, he drops his head, and skulks away to hide in comedic fashion. No matter what incentive is offered, he refuses point blank to look in the direction of the offending device.

Eventually, despite our challenges, I did fulfil my long-held ambition to take Doug to agility classes. We even signed up for the *fun* agility competition. As I dutifully walked the course with the other participants, who all seemed to be taking the *fun* event rather seriously, John set up his camping chair in a good spot to be a spectator. He happily soaked up the atmosphere, his enjoyment enhanced by the bottle of red wine he'd brought along. I did not partake. I was designated driver and also taking my duties as Doug's handler very seriously.

Our turn came and, with all eyes upon us, Doug and I entered the agility arena. I bent down to unclip his lead.

But rather than awaiting my command, he shot off like one of his Greyhound sisters at the height of her racing career. He bounced gleefully around the course. Paying no heed, whatsoever, to the actual order that the obstacles were supposed to be tackled in. He totally ignored my attempts at directing him, my waving arms and yelled commands were surplus to his requirements. He jumped, weaved, balanced, and ran around the course, thoroughly enjoying himself. Unfortunately, I tried but failed to match his spectacular speed. I lagged behind in a most undignified fashion.

Finally, Doug zoomed into the tunnel – one of his favourite bits of agility equipment. It was then I spied the club photographer poised and ready to get an action shot of Doug on exit. Predictably, Doug slammed on the brakes and froze midway. Puffing and panting I reached the tunnel with Doug still inside. At least this provided an opportunity for me to catch up. However, no amount of cajoling or coaxing would persuade Doug to exit the sanctuary of the tunnel and face the scary camera.

The other contestants were getting impatient at the hold up in proceedings, so I had no option but to go in after him. I crawled in on all fours to retrieve my dopey dog.

We made the show's website for all the wrong reasons. To my dismay, for all to see, was a very unflattering photo of my arse sticking out of the bright blue tunnel while a trainer held the other end aloft trying, unsuccessfully, to tip Doug out.

Like Doug, John had thoroughly enjoyed himself. On the way home he was in stitches. 'Did you have *fun* at the *not-much-fun* agility competition?'

It was an in-joke. John loved to ridicule anything with *fun* in the title. He called fun runs *'not-much-fun'* runs and referred to novelty bars of confectionary as *'not-much-fun'* size.

All our previous dogs had been so well-behaved that I'd been under the mistaken assumption I was gifted as some kind of a dog whisperer. But Doug was living proof of how incorrect this belief was.

Re-opening the door to the police officers, I immediately went on a charm offensive, defending my pack.

The Greyhounds had long-passed and we had a mis-matched crew of four: Doug; Chloe, a Collie type originally from France; Lil; and Olivia, a beautiful Lassie look-alike Rough Collie who, as a breeding bitch, had spent most of her life confined to a dog crate until she was rescued.

'They're a bit noisy but they're all harmless.' I raised my voice in order to be heard over the din, which even through my office door was still quite loud.

In that moment, I was blissfully unaware that life as I knew it had ended and that a living nightmare was about to begin.

The officers asked to come in and followed me along the hall, past the office containing the still barking dogs, into the living room.

'Is there anyone else in the house with you?'

'No.' *What's that got to do with barking dogs?*

'Do you know John Collins?'

Oh no, I thought, *what's he got up to now?* 'He's my husband,' I replied.

'There's been an… incident. At Kelvedon Station.'

'Incident?' *John hadn't been going to the station. He'd been driving to work.*

'I'm sorry to tell you this. I'm afraid he's deceased.'

The muscles in my face contorted with shock and pain. My legs buckled. I landed back on the sofa.

Staring at these strangers, these aliens so totally out of place in my home, I could not make sense of what they were telling me. From what sounded a long way off, I heard my voice pierce the white noise flooding my head, roaring so loud it obliterated every other sound, even the barking dogs.

I was screaming.

2

THE MEETING OF TWO

The meeting of two personalities is like the contact of two chemical substances: if there is any reaction, both are transformed.
Carl Jung

JOHN and I met way back in 1985 at a spit and sawdust body-building gym in South London. It was a testosterone-fuelled atmosphere, female members were in the distinct minority, and it had none of the finesse gyms have these days. It was an odd place. Almost noone paid the full fees. And everyone smoked cigarettes in the changing rooms before training. It was a different world back then.

I didn't see John as a potential boyfriend. We were friendly, we chatted and had a bit of a laugh, but that was about it. In fact, I had my eye on his friend, who was loud and flash. John seemed more reserved.

One day John asked if I'd give him a lift home from the gym, explaining his bicycle had a puncture. I drove a white Vauxhall Viva with baggy seatbelts, light blue leather seats, loads of rust, and a dodgy starter motor that frequently cut out at the most inconvenient times. I had to sit on a cushion to see out of the windscreen and, as it lacked a radio, I balanced a cassette player on the dashboard, which would often end up on the floor if I took a corner too sharply.

When we got to where John said he wanted to go, he thanked me and got out of the car, but then he hesitated. Leaning in through the still-open passenger door he asked, 'Got time for a quick drink?'

'Why not?' I said after only the briefest pause. His face broke into a beaming smile and he jumped back in the car beside me.

We hit it off right away. He was funny and kind. And pretty much from that day on, we were together.

I was twenty-three. John was twenty-seven.

When we met he was doing casual jobs. I was a single parent, unemployed but studying with a view to applying for teacher training.

Years later John confessed to making up the story of the flat tyre. Asking for the lift had just been a ploy to get me on my own. He'd actually chained his bike up round the corner from the gym. That way, if I'd said no to the lift, he wouldn't have to walk home.

Soon after we met, we were in a rowing boat on a lake in one of the London parks with Jake, my three-year-old son from my previous marriage.

'Having cancer,' John said, 'taught me not to worry so much.'

John's head of soft curls wasn't the result of some dubious fashion choice as my mum had pondered.

'Never imagined you'd fancy with a bloke with a perm!'

It was the result of chemotherapy. He'd shown me photos of him with the telltale chemo-induced bald head.

'They offered me a wig. I asked if they had a big, fuzzy, ginger one. You know, the type clowns wear. But they said the NHS didn't offer that as an option, so I politely declined.' John was full of one-liners and anecdotes.

'Worry is pointless,' he continued. 'If you've got a problem and you can do something about it, then do it. But if you can't do anything, there's no point worrying.' It was a philosophy John not only talked but walked.

I accompanied him to one of his routine post-cancer check-ups at Guy's Hospital. Looking around the waiting room at the other patients, he leaned close to me and whispered in my ear, 'Let's play spot the wig.'

His sense of humour was never unkind but it was often irreverent, even in sombre situations – like the waiting room of the cancer department.

When we met, I'd never been out of the UK. I didn't even own a passport. During the evenings when he came to see me after I'd put Jake to bed, John told mesmerising tales of meeting Bedouin nomads in the Sinai dessert, of floating on the Dead Sea, living with hippies in Jerusalem, and snorkelling in the crystal clear waters of Sharm El Sheikh. None of the other guys I'd dated before had been on such adventures.

'You're a Catholic, so how'd you end up living on a kibbutz?' I wanted to know.

John told me how it all started one day in his local pub in Bermondsey. A friend said he was planning to spend time volunteering on a kibbutz. John was between jobs and had no other commitments. Seeking an adventure, he decided to go too. John, his twin brother Jim, and their younger brother Vinny joined the friend and eventually all travelled to Israel together.

The stories he told of their adventures involved alcohol, girls, and good times. They were probably embellished and always had a great punchline. John could make a funny story out of anything, no matter how serious. Like the time he got shot at for inadvertently straying across the Egyptian-Israeli border. Or when his brother Vinny, who couldn't swim, was thrown in a swimming pool, ending up in hospital on the day he was supposed to be flying home. There was also the time John marched stark-naked into the dining room full of other kibbutz workers to collect his weekly wages. He did it just to prove a point: that the person who paid them never actually looked up from his desk. And he relished telling the tale of having sex with a female Israeli solider and being impressed by the size of her gun.

'You're a bit of a dark horse, aren't you?' When I'd met him in the gym I had no idea what a colourful life he'd led.

John smiled and shrugged. He never showed off about anything. He hated people pretending to be something they were not or bragging excessively about supposed achievements. John was quite the opposite. He was understated and full of surprises. The fact he was the kind of person who jumped at the opportunity to do something a bit different was exciting to me.

'You have to remember,' he chuckled, 'one of my jobs at the kibbutz was taking care of the hens – not so exciting. I spent a lot of time up to my knees in chicken shit.'

'You've never got any food.' John stared into the abyss of my empty fridge. He was strong, muscular, into his body building, and always hungry.

'Haven't got any money,' I replied.

Following that conversation, whenever John came to visit, he always arrived with a carrier bag of food plus a pack of cigarettes for me and sweets for Jake.

The first time he took me to the supermarket and paid for all the shopping was epic. I felt like a kid at Christmas as I admired all the groceries piled up at the checkout. As a single parent I was used to checking the price of everything before I put it in my basket. I usually stuck to buying the essentials. On this occasion, as I picked up each item and before I put it in the trolley, I asked, 'Can we have this?'

'You can have whatever you want. I love how happy it makes you simply to buy food.'

I felt like the luckiest girl alive. I had a gorgeous, generous man who wanted to take care of me and my son.

John and I never actually decided to live together. That is, we never really had a conversation about it. He just kind of moved in one possession, one item of clothing, at a time.

John proved himself a terrific stepdad to my little boy. He always treated Jake like his own son. Our first Christmas together, John spoiled three-year-old Jake with gifts: Thomas the Tank Engine, He-Man, and even the must-have toy of that year – a Castle Grayskull. All of these gifts John bought without being asked and without asking.

When John and I got together, my parents were worried I'd get side-tracked and abandon my studies and ambitions to better my life.

When I got pregnant so soon, which we did actually plan, they felt their initial concern was justified. In fact, they refused to talk about the pregnancy or the impending arrival of the little one at all. They didn't believe my protestations that I would never give up on my education and deep desire to improve my life. I was even more determined than ever because I would soon have two children.

3

THREE BECOME FOUR

JOHN and I got married in November 1986 at Camberwell Register Office in Southwark. It was an informal affair. The only guests were our respective parents, Jim, John's twin, their younger brother Dave who has special needs, and of course my son, Jake. Both our dads signed the register as witnesses. And Jake misbehaved because he wasn't the centre of attention. It was a simple day filled with love and fun.

Phoebe Florence was born the following month – December 1986. We named her Phoebe because it was unusual (way before the days of *Friends* on TV) and Florence after my grandmother, my dad's mum.

My heart melted as I watched John proudly cradling our newborn baby girl for the first time.

'Back when I was going through chemotherapy, I never imagined I'd be a dad.' John pulled his eyes away from his daughter's face to meet mine. 'I know everyone thinks their own baby is beautiful but she really is, isn't she?'

And of course she was. A little doll with pale skin and blue eyes.

When I was pregnant and first discovered I was having a girl, I'd been a bit disappointed. I loved having a son and wanted a brother for Jake. Plus, all the little girls my friends had were whiny creatures who cried and moaned at the drop of a hat. But from the moment she was born, I could not have been happier to be the proud mother of a daughter.

The first night we took her home, John was introduced to the reality of having a baby. We went to bed and put her down in the little wooden cradle next to our bed. But she just wouldn't settle. John looked at me with that haggard parent-of-a-newborn expression and over the din of her cries said, 'How are we supposed to sleep?'

I rolled my eyes and smiled. 'We don't! At least not until she does.'

When I was pregnant, my sister had said she thought Jake would be jealous of the new baby. He had, after all, been the centre of everyone's attention for four years and he totally loved it. But he took Phoebe's arrival in his stride and assumed the role of big brother. We were a complete little family: husband, wife, son, and daughter.

But when she was just days old, Phoebe got really sick. Her eyes started to roll back in her head and her little body became floppy. She deteriorated very quickly.

It was December and the kind of cold where your fingers go numb even when you're wearing woolly gloves. We left Jake with my parents, wrapped Phoebe up, and rushed to Kings College Hospital, which was literally across the road from our home.

The glow from the street lamps shimmering across the wet pavement outside was a stark contrast to the harsh florescent light inside the Accident and Emergency department.

Seeing how poorly our tiny baby was, we were quickly transferred to the children's ward. After the panic and first flurry of activity, we were put into a dimly lit side room. It was late and suddenly everything was very quiet.

I was worried about Jake. He was still only four and I wanted him to be tucked up safe in his own bed. So we decided John would collect him from my parents and take him home. Which is why I was alone with Phoebe when the doctor returned.

'We're unsure exactly what's wrong with your baby,' he said. 'It's obvious she's very unwell, so we have to do another test. It's quite invasive but should give us a clear picture of what's going on.'

My stomach lurched. 'What test?'

'It's called a lumbar puncture. We insert a needle into her spine and extract some cerebrospinal fluid.' His description was professional and his tone reassuring but as I looked at Phoebe, so little, her skin so white it was almost translucent, I flinched at the thought of a needle being stuck into her tiny spine.

This was long before the days of mobile phones so I had no way of contacting John. I agreed to the procedure. I wasn't allowed to be with her during the test.

Reluctantly I handed her over and watched a nurse carry her away down the corridor. There was nothing I could do except wait. And hope.

When the nurse brought Phoebe back to me, a special mat was placed underneath her tiny body inside the cot.

'It's wired up to this alarm,' the nurse informed me. 'If her heart or breathing stops, the alarm will beep.'

The alarm went off several times during that night. Each time, a nurse would rush in to check her and turn off the alarm. Seeing my obvious distress, one nurse reassured me, 'Sometimes it goes off just because she's moved and the mat can't detect a heartbeat. I tell you what, let's not bother with this. She seems okay. Why don't you just hold her.'

I was so relieved and grateful to have her back in my arms. I stroked her little feet trying to keep her awake. I was filled with terror. Convinced that if she went to sleep she wouldn't wake up. When finally she couldn't keep her eyes open any longer, and my arms ached almost as much as my heart, I placed her back in the see-through hospital cot and crouched next to it so I could watch the rise and fall of every shallow baby breath.

Thankfully, she made a full recovery from what turned out to be a nasty viral infection. But at the time, I had no idea this would not be the only hospital stay for Phoebe, with me at her side.

That festive season was Phoebe's first and our first as a family of four. We had a quiet Christmas with my parents and declined an invitation to a New Year's Eve party. John and I were more than content to stay home, grateful our little family were safe and well.

When Phoebe was about eighteen-months-old, the four of us were on holiday on the island of Majorca. My first time on an aeroplane and in a 'foreign' country had been when Phoebe was just a few months old. This was our second family holiday. While at a beach one day I was watching the kids play in the sand. Phoebe toddled off just a little farther away and then turned. She appeared to be looking in our direction but her expression seemed puzzled.

'John, I don't think she can see us.'

John and his twin brother Jim were both born with congenital cataracts. But this was the first time I'd considered Phoebe might have inherited them too.

John and his brother were sent to a special school for blind and partially sighted children. John's eyesight was not as poor as Jim's but, as they were twins, they were treated the same.

Among the 'normal' kids in the neighbourhood, the reputation of the school was that it was for 'backward' children. They were unkind and jeered at the kids in the playground. John found it all humiliating. Even as an adult, John remained deeply embarrassed about his school. If he ever had to tell anyone what school he attended, he would lie saying he went to the local comprehensive.

In typical John style, he told me funny stories about his school days. Including the one about the ringing football! In a darkly comedic fashion, making fun of himself rather than anyone else, he told elaborate tales of how they had a specially adapted ball with bells inside, so the kids who couldn't see at all could play along with those who could.

In spite of his jokes, however, I sensed he felt he'd been disadvantaged and that he might have got a better education in a mainstream school. The prospect of Phoebe following in his footsteps in this regard was heartbreaking for John.

As Phoebe was still so young, the only way for her eyes to be thoroughly examined was under general anaesthetic. With her screams of distress as background accompaniment, apparently not uncommon when babies have a 'general', solemnly, the doctor confirmed she had congenital cataracts in both eyes. We were told it was unlikely our daughter would be able to attend a mainstream school, drive a car, or do many of the things most of us with average eyesight take for granted.

Years of hospital visits followed. She was referred to Moorfields, a specialist NHS hospital in London, the oldest and largest centre for ophthalmic treatment, teaching, and research in Europe. We took Phoebe for regular checkups but resisted the recommended surgeries, influenced by John's memories of the horrible experiences he'd had as a child. Together we decided to wait until Phoebe was old enough to be fully informed of what was happening and could participate in the decisions.

4

AND THEN THERE WERE FIVE

WE WERE LIVING in a new-build maisonette in Ashworth Close, Camberwell, South East London. It was social housing, but really high quality, in a good area and with nice neighbours. In a material sense we didn't have much, but life was good. I was offered part time paid work at the adult education institute where I had originally volunteered. John had done some labouring for my dad, who was a self-employed plumber, and he encouraged John to go to college to get qualified himself. John was more than happy to do this. He loved working with my dad and was pleased to be given the opportunity to gain a skilled trade. He and my dad became firm friends. John would tell me stories of the building site banter they shared.

'There's a side to your dad you know nothing about,' he'd tease. I guess that's true of most people.

John loved going for breakfast in the greasy-spoon cafés with my dad and the other workers. My dad had a reputation for being a moaner and would cause mischief by complaining loudly about the poor quality of the cooking. Until one day the 'chef' appeared. A great hulking man, in a greasy vest, brandishing a spatula. Much to the amusement of their co-workers, he told my dad in a menacing way that if the menu didn't suit him, he could go elsewhere!

One day at work, John hid my dad's beloved tin of Golden Virginia tobacco. The other workers assured my dad they had no idea where it was and watched him searching in vain for his smokes, whooping and laughing when he finally spotted the tin, which John had nailed to the ceiling.

Those days in Ashworth Close with Jake and Phoebe were very happy.

After Phoebe came along, John and I moved into the smaller bedroom and put the kids in the larger one. John was great at all things DIY. He reconfigured the master bedroom into two by cleverly building wardrobes across the middle of the room. It created distinct spaces and the illusion, at least, of two bedrooms. One for Jake, one for Phoebe. One painted a vibrant *dinosaur* green, the other bright pink. It might not have been perfect, but we did the best we could and the space worked pretty well.

We had a big fish tank on the dresser in the kitchen. Nothing fancy, just cold water fish, so no need for expensive filters or heaters. After we put the kids to bed, sometimes John and I would reject the TV in favour of sitting side-by-side to watch the fish. We'd drink tea and discuss their antics. There were a couple of vibrant coloured Fantails and a couple of bug-eyed Black Moors. These graceful creatures would swim about serenely like models on a catwalk displaying flowing gowns.

There was also a sucker type of creature that didn't do much. Apparently it was supposed to keep the algae under control. And there were a few really skittish ones. I don't remember what breed they were. They swam really fast, racing about frantically, whizzing up and down the length of the tank. Every so often, for no apparent reason, one of them would get spooked and leap out of the water, ending up on the hard tiled floor, where it would madly flip and flop, gills flapping. I found this unspeakably disturbing. I could not bear to see the poor creature suspended between life and death. I would literally leap from my seat and flee from the room, refusing to return until John had scooped it up and popped it back into the safety of the tank. Sometimes they would be fine, carrying on as if nothing had happened. Sometimes the trauma of the event would prove too much and the next morning they would be floating lifeless on the surface of the water.

After a while working at the adult education institute, I was turned down for a promotion because I wasn't a graduate. When it became apparent my future prospects were limited, I applied to study for a degree as a mature student. I decided against the narrow vocational path of teaching, instead opting for a BSc (Hons) in Social Sciences, which would open up more options.

When I first received the letter offering me an unconditional place at the South Bank Polytechnic, which later became South Bank University, imposter syndrome set in. I didn't tell anyone about it for days, convinced there had been some mistake.

Before I embarked on my undergraduate degree course at South Bank, John bought me a book on how to study. On the cover it had an illustration of a figure modelled on Rodin's *The Thinker*, only holding a book.

Inside John had written: *To Denise, with this amazing book, college will be a piece of cake, love John.*

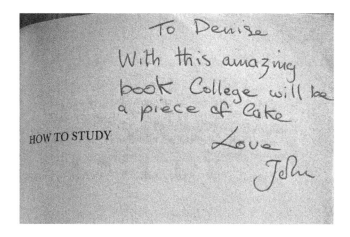

Studying full-time for a degree as a married woman with two young children was hard work. But I absolutely loved it. Especially the first year.

I adored spending time in the library, the lectures enthralled me, the seminars were thought provoking, and I even enjoyed the homework assignments. My dad promised that if I successfully completed my foundation year he would buy me a word processor. He was good to his word and I became the proud owner of an Amstrad with spell check. A total godsend for a dyslexic like me.

As time went on, and the work got harder, I became more stressed. The other students had no outside responsibilities. I was different, so felt like a bit of an outsider. Although Jake had started school, and John's mum kindly looked after Phoebe until we could place her in a community nursery in Peckham, it was all a bit of a struggle. I often felt short of time. Like I was rushing everything and always thinking of what I had to do next. The juggling act of full-time study, childcare, and constantly being short of money eventually caught up with me.

'You've possibly got a stomach ulcer, probably stress induced,' the doctor said. 'Let's run some tests and find out what's going on.'

A week or so later, as instructed, I phoned the doctor's surgery to get the results.

'Congratulations, Mrs Collins,' the receptionist said, her voice bright and cheery.

I was confused. Since when did having an ulcer warrant congratulations?

'It's positive. You're pregnant.'

That night as John soaked in the bath after a hard day's work, I went in and took a seat.

'I'm pregnant.'

Neither of us said anything for what felt like ages. We just looked at each other. Then John, with slow comedic timing, sank beneath the water until fully submerged. When he resurfaced, he spurted water from his mouth like a whale.

'Right.'

That night as we lay in bed, he said, 'So then, what do you want this time, a boy or a girl?'

'I'm not sure I can cope with another one,' I replied honestly.

It was still dark outside when we arrived at the maternity unit in the early hours of 18th November, 1989.

'Are you having another contraction?' John asked casually.

I was bent double and panting, gripping the edge of the bed. 'It's like you're psychic! Your powers of observation are so amazing,' I hissed between pains.

'Don't like to assume,' John shrugged.

The sun rose over the city and the delivery room, which was high up in the tower at King's College Hospital, flooded with the beautiful glow of radiant orange and yellow.

Liam James Albert Collins – James after John's twin brother and Albert after my uncle, Auntie Olive's husband – arrived at 11:15 a.m. Phoebe had been born at 11:15 p.m.

In the minutes after he entered the world, Liam opened his eyes and looked quizzically and directly at everyone in the delivery room.

The midwife smiled. 'I don't think it's the first time this one has been here.'

Liam was a beautiful baby with the biggest blue eyes. From day one he was content, with a curious yet knowing personality.

During the pregnancy, John and I came to the conclusion childcare would be impossible for three. The only way we could see it would be possible for me to complete my degree was for him to give up working with my dad and stay at home to care for the children. So after the Christmas break I returned to my studies, leaving John to be a house-husband.

With three children and two bedrooms, space soon became an issue. In those days, if you lived in social housing and you wanted to move, a proactive approach was to find someone to swap with. There were ways you could advertise what you had and what you were looking for. Once both sets of tenants agreed, so long as everyone was up-to-date with the rent, the process was fairly straightforward.

Our home in Ashworth Close was an attractive proposition. The location was prime, it was only a few years old, nicely maintained, and beautifully decorated. The woman who wanted to swap with us was living alone in a large four bedroomed house. It was in a terrible state of repair but the real issue was that John and I had reservations about the neighbourhood. It was only a few miles from where we lived, but in character it might as well have been a world away. Still, seduced by the prospect of so much space, we convinced ourselves it would be okay.

It wasn't.

5

THE HELL HOLE

EVEN AT THE tender age of ten, Leroy had the mean, no-neck, broad-shouldered look of a hard man in the making. This one was trouble. Jake, on the other hand, was soft – a dreamer, artistic, and desperate to belong. Up to that point he'd spent his entire life playing in the safety of communal gardens with kids whose parents all knew each other.

'Can Jake come out to play?' Leroy asked when I opened the door.

I shuddered at the thought of my son playing out with this thug. What did *playing out* even mean in this neighbourhood? I glanced out of the kitchen window at the view of inhospitable grey concrete blocks daubed with sprawling graffiti.

I checked myself. Leroy was only ten. Was I overreacting? I felt caught between a rock and a hard place. If I refused, would it make Jake's life more difficult? If I agreed, what might happen?

Jake returned home sporting a nice black eye, reticent to reveal the reason for the fight with Leroy.

A few days later, it transpired they had stolen stuff from a local newsagent's shop. Incensed, and probably a bit guilty I'd not just said no to the request to play out, I headed for Leroy's house.

In spite of the knot in the pit of my stomach, I pretended to be as formidable as I presumed Leroy's mother to be. Through the gaps between the slats of the weathered grey wooden gate, I could see her and Leroy in their tatty garden.

Her face was like thunder as I told her my version of events. Turning to go back to my house, I almost felt sorry for Leroy as I heard the way she yelled at him.

But it wasn't just the likes of Leroy that made our time in the hell hole so depressing. It was everything. The innocent looking little girl from next door who would come in to play with Phoebe and steal her toys. The gangs of teenagers who threw things at the windows every single night, not hard enough to actually break the glass but enough to be intimidating. The failed attempt to set fire to my car. The used needles left on the path by junkies who congregated in the stairwell of the flats right opposite our house. The packs of dogs roaming free and fouling everywhere. Having to say to the kids, 'Let's not walk to school that way this morning,' if the drunks who slept rough were getting aggravated over the last tin of Tennent's extra strong lager.

One time we took the kids away for a break to a holiday camp. It was basic but heavenly. Preparing for our return, my mum visited to make sure the house was clean and we had food in the fridge.

Knowing we wouldn't be happy at returning, she planted a pretty basket of colourful trailing flowers and green plants, and my dad put up a metal hanger for it by the front door. In the short space of time between my parents' departure and our arrival, vandals ripped the flowers and plants from the basket, stuffing them and the soil they had been lovingly planted in, through letterbox. They smashed the basket on the ground and bent the hanger.

This mindless, senseless act of destroying any attempt to improve things summed up the character of the place and most of the people living there.

February 1991, John got an unexpected call. His dad had suffered a stroke and was in the hospital asking for John. He dropped everything and rushed off. Hours later, when he returned, I could see he'd been crying. He didn't say a word, just shook his head and I knew his dad was gone. We stood and held each other for a long time.

John was badly affected by the loss of his father. He was just so sad. He told me his dad's death had not been peaceful. There were things he had wanted to say to him but never got the opportunity. One night in bed he cried again. 'He's just gone. Where do you think he is?'

'I don't know.' Although John had been raised Catholic, neither of us believed in an afterlife. So, I could offer no words of comfort about him being in a better place now. John wanted to make love. 'Do you think it's wrong to want to?'

'Of course not.'

John needed tenderness and reassurance and I gave it to him. Life goes on.

Looking at the intricate floral tributes at the funeral, I couldn't help but think, *What a waste of money.* I wished we'd spent the money on him while he was alive rather than on flowers he'd never see.

John didn't cry at the funeral.

My graduation was one joyful event during an otherwise pretty bleak time in The Hell Hole. The ceremony was in Southwark Cathedral. I'm only five feet two inches, but I walked a little taller that day, proud of everything the gown and mortar board represented. John and my dad, both suited and booted, were my guests. Mum stayed home to look after Jake, Phoebe, and Liam. Waiting with all the other graduates at the front of the cathedral to collect my degree from the chancellor, I worried they might be bored by the pomp of the occasion and the length of the ceremony.

It isn't the official photograph that Dad paid for, that I treasure. It's a snapshot of me and John standing outside the cathedral, John young and handsome, me steadying the mortar board on my head.

Not long after graduation, I was delighted to get a job working for a local branch of a nationwide charity. It supported people with life limiting conditions and their carers. I was so desperate to get the position of deputy co-ordinator that at the interview, when they asked if I had any questions, I said, 'What question do I need to ask to make you offer me the job?'

Val, the co-ordinator, was well educated and nurturing. She guided my professional development and I flourished. Eagerly, I undertook a lot of in-service training, including a management qualification and counselling courses.

Meanwhile, John and I continued to plan our escape, which involved looking for another local authority swap.

We desperately hoped we would end up somewhere better. It was hard to imagine anywhere worse. John was like a man possessed. He worked tirelessly to renovate the whole house, every room unrecognisable by the time he finished. He'd work late into the night, every night. At first it was an attempt to make the inside of the spacious house as nice as possible, to detract from the horrible neighbourhood. But once we realised that no matter how lovely we made the interior, it was still a nightmare to live there, the focus shifted to making it irresistible to anyone looking for a swap.

I couldn't shake the dread that we were stuck in this awful place forever. Who in their right mind would want to move to here? I'd lost sight of how beautiful the house was thanks to John's efforts. I didn't fully appreciate that it was located in London and that people living outside the capital might be eager to move into the city.

'I promise you,' John said. 'I will get us out of here.'

I had no idea how he'd fulfil that promise but I trusted him. Just hearing him say those words, with such conviction, made me feel a little better.

We were having Sunday lunch when I took a phone call about a potential house swap. The man on the other end of the line had a strong accent. When I asked him where the house was that he wanted to swap, it sounded like he said, 'Grey Burrow, Chelmsford. In Essex.'

John retrieved the big map book from the car. Long before we had a sat nav, we used that map book to navigate all our days out, our trips to theme parks, zoos, events, the coast, and our holidays. I peered over John's shoulder as we searched the index but could find no 'Grey Burrow'. Opening the map at the page showing Chelmsford, we found Great Baddow, a suburb on the outskirts of the town. We agreed that must be it.

We later discovered the man I'd spoken to on the phone, and his family, were refugees. They were eager to move to London to be nearer their community and to live in an area offering more diversity than Great Baddow did in those days. We arranged a time for them to visit. It was immediately obvious how impressed they were by the high standard of the interior of the house. And they were delighted it was large enough for their whole family to be together.

The first time John and I visited Great Baddow we went on our own, without the children. I was sceptical. 'First sign of an abandoned shopping trolley or a burnt out car and we're out of here.' We looked at each other and burst out laughing.

The house, built in 1919, was a three-bedroom mid-terrace, with a small dining room and a decent sized lounge. It was in desperate need of a new kitchen and overall decorating but it was clean and tidy. The front and rear gardens were nice. After living in The Hell Hole for eighteen months, which John and I likened to serving a prison sentence, our main concern was the neighbourhood. We knew that no matter how nice a house could be made inside, it can't make up for an inhospitable area.

At that time, Chelmsford was a quiet town where all the shops still closed on Sunday. It didn't even have a cinema. Great Baddow itself was lovely. Many of the terraced houses had pretty front gardens full of flowers and well kept lawns and hedges.

At the end of the road, on the way to the school Jake and Phoebe would attend, there was a recreation field. The school was a far cry from the grey concrete of London, boasting a playing field and a swimming pool. Within walking distance was a parade of shops called The Vineyards. It seemed a world away from The Hell Hole. John and I looked at each other. We felt like we had won the lottery. Great Baddow felt safe.

For a while after the move I continued to work in London. Sometimes I commuted. Sometimes I stayed over at my parents'. John set about renovating yet another house.

My parents, especially my mum, were heartbroken at us moving – what felt to them – a very long way away. But they knew how unhappy we'd been and how desperate we were to move.

Eventually, I got a job with the same charity at a branch in a nearby town. And John worked to establish himself as a local plumber. My parents followed us and also moved to Essex. As did my auntie Olive, and my sister.

Phoebe had her first surgery just before she went up to high school. She had not been given the help or support she deserved at junior school. Her poor sight had negatively affected her confidence and she had been bullied. Perhaps we shouldn't have waited. Maybe if she'd had the surgery sooner it would have been better. But you do your best as parents. Only hindsight is 20-20. We hoped the surgery would improve things for her.

'Why can't she have both eyes done at the same time?' I asked at the pre-op assessment.

'There's always the possibility the operation will result in total loss of sight. So we operate on one eye at a time to minimise the risk of blindness.' The doctor slid the consent form across the desk for us to sign.

That first operation was a success. Although unpleasant, the procedure to remove the cataract and implant an artificial lens was straightforward. Phoebe's stay in hospital was okay, although I was shocked to see some of the other children on the ward. There was one poor little boy I will always remember. He had no eyes or eye sockets. His operation, to insert false eyes, was merely cosmetic to make his appearance more normal, more acceptable to others.

When it came to having the sutures removed from her eye, a process that was quite barbaric, Phoebe was really brave. A nurse used a needle to pick out the row of stitches holding together the wound around the new lens.

Some months later, we were back at Moorfields for the second operation. This time, things didn't go according to plan at all. Phoebe was hysterical with pain when she came round from the anaesthetic. Apparently, there were complications during the operation and the lens had to be removed and reinserted. In addition to the pain, this resulted in trauma to the eye and a permanent distortion to the pupil. Before the operation, Phoebe was a girl who wouldn't walk when she could cartwheel. After the operation, she had to give up her beloved gymnastics.

6

THE SUN ALWAYS SHONE

PHOEBE ONCE REMARKED that when she remembered outings from her childhood, it seemed as if the sun was always shining. I laughed. 'That's because, back in those days, if it was a really nice day, Dad and I would give you a day off school and we'd go on an outing.'

Parents could do that sort of thing back then without any real consequences. And so, if the weather was particularly good and John and I could wrangle a day off, rather than send them to school we'd go to a farm, a theme park, a castle, or the seaside instead. Hence her memories of long, hot sunny days. We had loads of fun times and adventures at weekends and school holidays too. We took them places and showed them things – from safari parks and zoos, to beaches, museums, and historical reenactments.

I'd always drive and John would invariably eat whatever picnic I had made long before we arrived at our destination.

Holidays were mostly spent in the UK. Often at holiday camps.

One of Phoebe's favourite photos is of her playing crazy golf with her dad at Pontins holiday camp.

The year it opened we went to Disneyland Paris. John's mum accompanied us and we had a magical time.

In spite of the long drive, Cornwall was a favourite destination. When the kids had a go at surfing, getting in and out of the wetsuits took far longer than the time spent in the water. John thought it would be funny to play a trick on me. So he encouraged the kids to dig a big hole in the sand and cover it with a beach towel. Unsuspecting, I sat down and promptly ended up with my feet in the air and my arse in the cold water which had filled the hole. They thought it was hilarious. I was less amused and went off to sulk in the car. Eventually John came to get me. Trying to keep a straight face, he offered a weak apology which ended with, 'You have to admit, it was funny.' I did not agree.

We have the obligatory photograph of us at Land's End, next to the signpost showing how many miles to home. The sun is indeed shining, and we are all smiling, the beautiful wild expanse of the sea in the background. While sitting on a cliff edge above that wild rocky coast, a bright red search and rescue helicopter flew past, seemingly almost at eye level, contrasting with the blue of the sea and sky.

We spent many hours in the car criss-crossing Bodmin Moor, through the narrow winding lanes on magical mystery tours (aka lost).

On a visit to the dark, dank Bodmin Jail, I read out tragic tales of long-dead inmates as the kids imagined what it would be like to be imprisoned there.

We visited sites of sacred standing stones and the museum of witchcraft with all its spooky exhibits. We enjoyed traditional cream teas, scones piled high with strawberry jam and thick clotted cream. Liam didn't drink tea and insisted on ordering Coke, transforming his cream tea into a 'Cream Coke'.

We searched out the Rocky Valley labyrinth carving. We rode the tractor around the Cider Farm orchard. We trekked through dense woodland, the kids running ahead, following the river until we came to the mysterious sacred site favoured by pagans, St Nectan's Glen. We paid our entrance fee and clambered down the steps to the damp, mossy site of the sixty-foot waterfall. High up, water burst through a circular hole in the rocks, created by the force of the water over many centuries. The kids paddled in the shallow pool at its foot while John and I soaked up the serenity.

We climbed the steep rock stairs cut into the cliffs of Tintagel Castle, set on the rugged north coast and, as legend suggests, the home of King Arthur. While the views of sea and wide-open sky were breathtaking, John, not a fan of heights, hung back tentatively from the edge. We listened to stories of the legendary magician Merlin and the Knights of the Round Table while the kids enjoyed the adventure and imagination of the place.

We all went pony trekking. No riding skill was required as the well-behaved ponies plodded along a route they knew well. It was fairly sedate until Liam's pony, Topper, decided to trot off on his own to explore what was on offer in a garden.

One year we hired a houseboat on the Norfolk Broads. It came with use of a small rowing boat in which the kids had all kinds of adventures, feeding the swans and catching frogs.

One day they badgered us to pay for canoe hire. This rapidly lost its allure as they realised how tricky it was to stay upright.

John and Jake had fishing rods. Almost every time John cast, he caught a fish, much to Jake's growing annoyance.

'I'm not even trying,' John shrugged apologetically as I told him to give Jake a chance.

 On returning from the local village with supplies, I saw great white clouds of smoke billowing from the back of the boat. As I got closer I could just make out John, his eyes streaming and arms waving, the kids laughing hysterically and jumping around. John had decided it would be nice to have a BBQ and had lit a disposable one at the back of the boat. But he'd managed to leave some of the packaging on, which had promptly caught fire. The rising heat had started to melt the paint off the underside of overhang.

On our final day on the houseboat, there was much hilarity as we drove away. John told us about a big dump he had taken in the boat's chemical toilet just before we left and we each contributed to ever more elaborate stories of the mighty dump being responsible for the sinking of the ship.

Through breathless giggles, we told tales of how the angry proprietor would pursue us, demanding additional money to pay for the boat to be raised from the deep, like the English warship the *Mary Rose*.

There were holidays further afield too. In hotter sunnier climes that involved kids clubs and mopeds. Trips in glass bottomed boats and excursions to various 'places of interest'.

Most of our days out and holidays were duly recorded on an enormous camcorder we carried with us, and they'd conclude with a trip to Grandma and Grandpa's – my parents – where there was always a plentiful supply of sweets and cake. We'd play the videos through the TV while recounting the highlights of that particular adventure, sharing every detail with them.

Like most parents, John and I did all we could to make Christmas a magical time for our children. From outings to see Santa to ensuring they got whatever the 'must have' present of the year was.

With three of them, and so much anticipation and excitement, they could keep each other awake very late on Christmas Eve. But once they were all sleeping, John and I would start wrapping the kids' main presents to put under the tree, which were from us, and preparing Santa stockings, which we'd sneak in and leave at the foot of their beds.

Santa brought the *stocking fillers*, which comprised a variety of smaller gifts and treats we knew the kids would love. They were allowed to open these as soon as they woke up on Christmas morning.

It often felt to us like we had only just closed our eyes and they were up and awake, squealing with delight at the array of things Santa had delivered. They'd come into our room, jumping on the bed, excited to show us all the gifts Santa had supplied. We'd act surprised and pretend we'd never seen any of the stuff before.

One Christmas morning, it felt somehow different. John and I could hear the kids all whispering to each other. From the snippets of their conversations we could make out that rather, than immediately ripping open the brightly coloured wrapping paper as they always did, they had decided for some reason to play at trying to guess what was in each parcel. We listened as they discussed all the potential possibilities, some quite outlandish, as they examined each wrapped stocking filler in turn. John and I tried to stifle giggles as we listened to the cuteness overload melting our hearts.

Although we would do most of the actual Christmas shopping together, it was mainly my responsibility, as Mum, to know what everyone wanted and ensure they got it. John would do the typical man thing; rushing out on his own on Christmas Eve to buy something for me.

One year he forgot Christmas.

On Christmas morning, he looked at me with an expression of utter confusion. 'I thought I had another day!' At first I thought it was a joke, certain there would be a punch line and a surprise.

But no. He had actually forgotten it was Christmas Day. He made up for it, big time, the following Valentine's Day though. He went totally over the top with presents: a pair of diamond earrings; a solitaire diamond ring; and a delicate gold watch. All wrapped in boxes within boxes, starting with an enormous box then descending down in size. There was a massive card too, in which he had written:

Am I forgiven for Christmas?

Christmas morning was always mayhem, with piles of presents and discarded wrapping paper covering the floor. I'd be fighting a losing battle trying to get the kids to eat something other than the entire contents of their chocolate selection boxes for breakfast. By late morning, we would all be ready to make the short journey to my parents' house for Christmas lunch and yet more presents.

My dad loved Christmas and went overboard with the decorations. The living room and conservatory resembled Santa's grotto. There was a tree and decorations from my childhood plus new ones added every year. And fairy lights everywhere. Dad believed it was impossible to have too many Christmas lights and each year he would attempt to outdo the previous display. He would greet us enthusiastically, a glass of sherry for the adults and bowls of sweets in bright wrappers for the kids. My mum would be fussing over whether the turkey was too dry or the gravy too thin. It was pretty much the same every year; a family affair with my parents, Auntie Olive, the kids, crackers, presents, and way too much food.

I'll aways remember the Christmas John decided to surprise us all by randomly dressing as Elvis. He appeared resplendent in a white jumpsuit with gold rimmed aviator shades, a distinctive jet black wig with accompanying mutton chop sideburns, carrying a microphone.

'Are you going to wear that all day?' my mother asked disdainfully as we sat down to Christmas lunch.

With a curl of the lip, John replied, 'Uh huh huh.'

Mum placed a plate, piled high with traditional Christmas food, on the table in front of him. In his best Elvis voice, he said, 'Why thank you, Mam. Thank you very much.'

It was a period of relative stability but because we aspired to improve our situation, we made the decision to take advantage of the 'Right To Buy' scheme and purchase our house in Great Baddow from the local authority. Money was often very tight but we did our best to shield the kids from the fact.

The inane music playing down the phone line did nothing to soothe my pounding head or heart. After what felt like an eternity someone answered. I could hear myself rambling as I attempted to explain my financial situation. Pleading with the faceless person who held my fate in her hands, my eyes scanned the innocent enough looking letter I still clutched. White page, black typeface, red logo. My words faded into an echoing void of unresponsive silence. I thought maybe the line had gone dead but no.

'I'm sorry Mrs. Collins,' her tone was curt, 'but the letter is correct. The bank needs full repayment of your overdraft by the end of the month.'

Unaffected by my hard luck story, there was no place for compassion in this exchange.

'But what am I supposed to do? I've had an overdraft facility on this account for ages.'

'And that is precisely the problem, Mrs. Collins. An *overdraft*...' Was I imagining her exaggeration of the word? 'An overdraft is intended merely as a buffer. You aren't supposed to live in it permanently.'

Every month, for as long as I could remember, my wages had been immediately swallowed by the black hole of this overdraft.

'Is there no way you can help me?'

I prayed the brief ensuing pause might be a pre-cursor of assistance.

'I can transfer you to someone in our loans department.'

The absurdity of the offer hung suspended in the air between us. I did not earn enough money to cover my monthly outgoings, hence reliance on the overdraft facility. A loan would mean even more debt and repayments would increase the monthly outgoings I already could not afford. For too long, stress caused by insufficient income had composed a dissonant soundtrack to my life.

The day was warm. Nice for sitting outside in my parents' garden. I tried to ignore the knot of anxiety in my stomach and focus instead on enjoying my tea. Mum always put the kettle on the moment anyone came through the door. Dad and I sat beneath the yellow and white awning, shaded from the sun. Behind us in the kitchen, the sounds of pots clanking and water swishing from the tap signalled Mum was content in her domestic domain and happy to stay out of our conversation.

Dad and I faced the bright vibrant garden rather than look directly at each other, even as we conversed. I glanced sideways at him. The sleeves of his bright blue shirt, the same shade as his eyes, were rolled up to his elbows. The customary braces contrasting in red were not a fashion accessory but purely functional; a means to hold up his trousers and frame his rotund belly. His skin was the colour of rich brown sugar. The result of spending every possible daylight moment outside. Still physically strong, the tan gave him a healthy glow that didn't tell the whole story. His COPD (Chronic obstructive pulmonary disease) forced him to sit down more these days.

He'd smoked heavily for forty years until, to everyone's surprise, he stopped. He'd favoured roll-ups, crafted from thin papers and shreds of rich brown pungent tobacco. There was a ritual to the whole process of creating these tightly rolled smokes with their untidy ends. Constantly burning out, they required regular re-lighting. He often kept one ready to go, saved for later, tucked neatly behind his ear. A tin of Golden Virginia tobacco always made the obvious gift for Father's Day, birthdays, and Christmas. As a child I hated the smell on his breath.

His brain still moved fast but sometimes his body or, more precisely, his lungs could not keep up. My eyes sketched the criss-crossed patterns of his wrinkles.

'The garden's looking good.' I stated the obvious and took another sip of tea. He huffed loudly, faking exasperation at the enormity of maintaining such a creation. Since retirement, the garden had become his surrogate job. It provided an ever-evolving, never ending project. A wasteland when my parents bought the place, gradually he had transformed the garden into this riot of shape, form, and colour. He'd designed and built a mini bandstand, a wishing well, and the humble garage was now 'pond cottage'. There were little water features constructed expertly from pipes and copper spouts, providing a constant soundtrack of flowing water that trickled, poured and splashed. Concealed at the very end of the garden, so as not to spoil the view, the washing line was tucked neatly out of sight. Not the most practical place for it, but then it wasn't his job to actually hang out the washing.

Previously, they had always lived in flats without gardens. Until I was eleven, we lived in a block grandly named Cutcombe 'Mansions'. Out the back was a concrete yard. There were deep, big, open drains, which dad covered with hardboard. He constructed a metal framed swing for me. Bleak as it was, as a little girl with a good imagination, I loved to play in that yard.

Dad and I had not always enjoyed the closest relationship. He was a good dad, he didn't do anything wrong, we just didn't always get along that well. My mum was probably partly responsible. It was like she feared there was a finite quantity of love in the world. If I loved Dad, then somehow the amount of love available for her would be diminished.

Dad's default mode was to say no to any request. Especially if it involved money. His caution was hardly surprising given his upbringing. He'd experienced the hardship of real poverty first-hand. Born in 1929, his early years were overshadowed by the Great Depression. He said the sight of desperate, jobless men standing in line outside the labour exchange would forever haunt him. His father had deserted his mother, leaving her to raise five children alone in the days before welfare benefits. Her only option was to prove herself one of the *deserving poor* and hope the assistance board would see fit to bestow charity.

Dad made an exception when it came to education. He regarded that as a good investment. He said, 'Once acquired, knowledge is one of the only things that can't be taken from you.'

Still looking out towards the garden rather than at me, he responded to my request.

'I could give you the money to pay off your overdraft.'

The glimmer of hope illuminating the darkness was short-lived.

'But that wouldn't help you in the long run. Fact is, if you're spending more than you are earning, that's unsustainable.'

I knew he was right but it felt like John and I just couldn't keep our heads above water and we were in real danger of drowning.

'You know I'll always lend you money if there's something specific you need.' And yes he always did – as long as I presented a strong case for said item, together with a solid plan of how I would repay the loan, he would always help with tangible things. But debt was different.

'Paying off your overdraft just won't help you.'

'Could we test your hypothesis?' I ventured. 'I'm pretty sure you're wrong.'

Although he smiled, I knew that was the end of the conversation.

Mum and Dad in their garden

7

CHEMICAL IMBALANCE

I'D BEEN HAVING a lot of bad headaches, so I went to see a doctor.

'The chemicals in your brain are out of balance,' the doctor declared. 'You're not producing enough serotonin.' He wrote out a prescription for Prozac, ripped the page from his notepad, and handed it to me.

'Depression like yours is a lifelong condition.'

It wasn't the first time I'd been 'diagnosed' with depression.

The first time was when I was about fourteen. My older sister had split from her first husband. Craving approval, love, and attention, and wanting to appear mature, I happily became her companion on nights out to meet guys. In those days, proof of age was never requested. It was far from unusual for underage girls and boys to drink in pubs and nightclubs, or discos as we called them back then.

A particular favourite of ours was the Sundowner on Tottenham Court Road. I loved dancing the night away in the dark smokey pubs and clubs. I didn't even mind that your feet stuck fast to the booze-soaked floor if you stood in the same place for too long; I'd been granted access to a wonderland where I was magically transformed into a pseudo-adult. The male attention I received appeared confirmation of my maturity.

I was too naïve to realise how inappropriate it all was. During these heady nights out I developed a taste for smoking, drinking, and sex. The man who took my virginity simultaneously broke my heart. I mistook his erection for true love, while he regarded the quick shag as a one-off. This experience of rejection was at the root of my low mood. But at the young age, how could I possibly tell the elderly GP, who knew my family and had known me all my life, what had really prompted the way I felt?

There was no reason to mention this previous diagnosis now. Back then I felt depressed because of what had happened. This time the doctor said it was to do with my brain. It didn't occur to me to ask why or how brain chemicals became 'out of balance'.

Why would I?

I simply accepted that brains go wrong. The explanation appeared biological, scientific, medical. I had depression like I had blue eyes. The diagnosis offered a kind of relief. Perhaps after all there was a simple way to not feel depressed. All I had to do was swallow the yellow and green capsules and they would magically make me feel better. *Like insulin for a diabetic*. It made perfect sense. It was a narrative I could get behind and endorse. Why would I question my GP? A trusted and authoritative source?

Throughout the years I would repeat the 'chemical imbalance' story to family, friends, colleagues, and eventually to clients.

'If you had a broken leg you would need a cast to help it heal. If you were diabetic, you wouldn't risk seeing how you'd get on without taking insulin,' I'd say, parroting a storyline I thought was rooted in proven science.

It was a rare treat for John and I to get away on our own. I vaguely recall we'd got a discounted stay at the hotel as some kind of an incentive when John signed up for a new mobile phone contract or something. It was only Surrey, the North Downs. Not a million miles away from home. But it was blissful.

We climbed Box Hill. It was that time of the day before the day has decided what kind of day it is going to be. Then the sun came out. Everything looked so green and the big wide open sky was so blue, with just the occasional wisp of white. The wind in the trees sounded strangely like the ocean. Conversations carried on the breeze meant we could hear the voices of other walkers but not make out their words. I was glad. I didn't want to have to engage with anyone else. It was lovely that it was just us. Just me and John.

Our conversation meandered and we talked about nothing of much importance, just the random subjects that crop up when you're with someone you know well. John told me all about The Ace Café, a favourite hangout for bikers. Although at the time John didn't own a motorcycle, he'd had bikes before we met and dreamed of one day owning a Harley Davidson. It was nice to just be together with nothing to worry about and noone to please or take care of. Except ourselves. We fantasised about staying on an extra night, knowing it wasn't possible as we'd left the kids with my mum and had to get back.

The hotel was renowned for its restaurant, although we didn't know that when we booked. The dinner had been amazing. And we drank a lot of red wine. John acted like we had all the money in the world and this was what we did every night. It was fun.

After dinner, feeling full and pleasantly drunk, we walked the streets of this lovely place for ages in an attempt to sober up a little and relieve our aching bellies.

The window display of a florist's shop caught our attention and we stopped. There was a statue of a huge green rabbit, standing on hind legs like a person, surrounded by garlands of flowers and other woodland creatures. It looked like something from a weird horror film. Although maybe that was because we were still a bit drunk. Laughing, we took turns making up scary names for it and tall tales of what it got up to. Finally we walked on, not really knowing or particularly caring where we were walking to.

'Do you think I seem different?' I asked.

'In what way?'

'Do I seem… happier?'

'Of course you're happy. We're on holiday!' John said, exaggerating the word holiday.

'I don't mean right now. I mean lately.' I still felt a bit of a bounce in my step, only now I was more conscious of the ground beneath my feet, even if it was too dark to see much of it. 'The doctor gave me these pills. Antidepressants.'

'How are they anti-depression? Do they give you a bigger bank balance?'

We both laughed but I wanted to tell John about what the doctor had said.

'They seem to take the edge off. You know, make me feel a bit more... able to chill out.'

'Like having a bottle of wine, you mean?'

'The doctor said it's all down to brain chemicals.'

'What?'

'Chemicals in the brain. If you get depressed it's like your brain doesn't make enough. He said the pills, for someone like me with depression, are like insulin for a diabetic.'

'But you're still going to have problems. That's just life.'

'Yes, I guess so,' I conceded. 'Do you mind? About the pills, I mean?'

'Of course I don't mind.'

John paused. 'It's not me, is it? Causing you to be depressed?'

I laughed. 'No, it's not you. I told you, it's a chemical imbalance. That's why I've got the pills. And the doctor has put me on a waiting list to speak to a counsellor.'

'Why do you need to see a counsellor if it's a chemical imbalance?'

It was a good question which I could not answer.

8

DO YOU WANT TO...?

AFTER WORKING at the charity for nine years, I was ready for a change. While reading through the job advertisements in a local newspaper, I saw an unusual ad for a training course. It said:

Do you want to be a self-employed hypnotherapist?

I have to confess that until that moment, the thought had never entered my head. However, the prospect of working for myself and making use of all the in-service counselling training I'd undertaken did appeal to me. I did my research on the course. We had a few heart-to-heart discussions about whether we could financially stretch to afford the fees, but as John's work as a self-employed plumber was regular, we agreed I should give it a go. I signed up to study for a diploma in cognitive and analytical hypnotherapy and psychotherapy.

The course was challenging and there were lots of times I sincerely doubted if I was up to it.

'Of course it's hard,' John said in his usual encouraging way. 'If it was easy, anyone could do it.' He always had more faith in my ability than I did.

I loved the course. The information and practical exercises were fascinating. I discovered a lot about myself and began to shift my perspective on a lot of things. Maybe I not only wanted to change career but was also looking for a way to 'cure' my depression?

The main tutor, an enigmatic character, made no hint of an apology for disagreeing with me when I trotted out the story that depression was caused by a chemical imbalance, and therefore required drugs to treat it.

'If everything comes from somewhere and nothing comes from nowhere,' he said in his strong Freud-like accent, 'then what actually *causes* the chemicals to become out of balance? Discover that and you discover why you are feeling depressed. A drug, at best will merely throw a cover over the problem.'

As I had the upmost respect for him, and I could not formulate a coherent argument, I decided to keep quiet about the fact I was taking antidepressants.

After successfully graduating the course, I left my job at the charity and set up as a self-employed therapist. I worked from our dining room, which had been transformed into my consulting room.

John, as ever, was amazingly supportive. Especially when it was tough going in the early days and I wondered if I had made the wrong decision leaving a salaried job to go self-employed.

'If you stop paying for advertising in order to save money,' he said, 'noone will know you're here and you won't get any clients.' John took over the payments for my advertising until my practice took off and I had a steady stream of regular clients.

As it turned out, it did not take too long for my practice to really take off. Soon I was earning more money than I ever had before. For the next five years, I worked one-to-one with a variety of clients. John, the kids and myself all benefitted from the increase in our family income. Life got a lot easier and our Christmas gifts and holidays got a bit of an upgrade.

9

TRUTH AND LIES

I WAS BRUSHING MY HAIR, standing in front of the mirror in our bedroom. John came up behind me, slipped his arms around my waist, and leaned his chin on my shoulder. He looked at me through the mirror

'Are we all right?' he asked.

I drew a deep breath and turned to face him.

'No,' I said, shaking my head. I kissed him and continued. 'We are not all right, not yet. But we will be.'

We'd been out one evening not long before this, celebrating my birthday. John came back from the toilet, sat down at the table, and said he had something to tell me.

'You know how you thought I messed around? You know, been unfaithful?'

I'd had my suspicions and raised them several times. But he had always laughed them off and said I was crazy.

A jolt of anxiety shot through me, and I felt sick.

'Well,' John continued, looking down, twisting the fork in his hand. 'You were right. It was years ago but I was unfaithful on more than one occasion and with more than one woman.'

This was surreal. I had no idea what to say, so remained silent.

'It wasn't because I didn't love you,' John continued, 'and it wasn't because I didn't find you attractive. Because I always did – do – on both counts.'

He was looking right at me and I could see the tears in his eyes.

'It was simply because I could. The opportunity presented itself and I went for it. And I am really, really sorry.'

My stomach hit the floor. I was stunned. In that one moment, by finally being honest, John had confirmed he could not be trusted.

'How could you do that to me?' I finally asked.

'At the time,' his face transparent as glass, he replied, 'I wasn't thinking about you.'

We spent the rest of that night in heart-wrenching conversation. We were both upset. I told John, in no uncertain terms, that I really didn't know if I could see a future for us.

The next morning, John got up, got dressed, and left the house without saying anything. He was gone for days.

We reported him missing to the police. I, the kids, my parents, and John's family were at our wits' end. Dad took Liam to the cinema to see a Rowan Atkinson comedy, trying to take his mind off things. It was Phoebe who finally thought of where John might have gone. We told the police and they found him. When I finally picked him up at Chelmsford railway station to bring him home, it transpired he'd spent days drinking heavily and had swallowed a pack of paracetamols. He claimed it had been a miserable cry for help rather than a serious attempt at suicide.

I was livid that he could put the kids through such a trauma. Phoebe was due to take her GCSE exams at school. Jake was working his first job as a lifeguard at the local pool after leaving school. And Liam was still just a little boy. I insisted John go to the local accident and emergency department to seek advice about the potential long-term effects of the paracetamol. It was more an attempt to make him face up to the severity of the situation but, as expected, the doctor confirmed it was unlikely to have any adverse effect. On John's medical notes it was listed as an impulsive act prompted by our argument rather than the result of any mental health issues.

John and I talked frankly and openly about the reasons he'd gone missing. Eventually I sought therapy to help me deal with what had happened, and to find ways to try to improve our relationship. I suggested perhaps John might also benefit from seeing a therapist.

'Why do I have to see someone else? Can't I just talk to you? You're a therapist.'

'I might be *a therapist*, but I am *your wife*. I can't be both.'

John thought about it for a while but then did arrange to go to see a private relationship counsellor to talk things over. The sessions he went for seemed to help him feel a bit better about it all. He never said much about what specifically was discussed. Except once he told me the counsellor had said, 'John, why do you feel so guilty? So, you fucked someone else. It's hardly a war crime.'

The comment angered me. I was doing a great job of playing the hard-done-by victim. The innocent, cheated-on wife. Later, I came to understand John's counsellor was simply, if a little provoca-tively, attempting to put things into perspective so John could see a way to get through the crushing guilt he felt, which is not a healthy emotion to carry.

John and I also attended a personal development course together, which was useful for bringing us closer. After one of these group sessions, in the car driving home, he began talking about incidents from his childhood that stuck with him.

'I got given this bicycle. I think for my birthday or maybe it was Christmas.' John was looking out the passenger side window as I drove. 'I was about six or seven. I loved it. It was the best thing ever. One day I had it. Then it was gone. No explanation. Nothing. It just disappeared.'

I glanced over at him then back to the road. He continued. 'But I knew it was my dad who had taken it. I don't know if he had to give it back because he couldn't afford the payments, or if he sold it. Noone ever said anything. It just disappeared. That wasn't the only time a present disappeared like that. And it wasn't only my things either.'

I resisted the urge to say something and just kept driving, waiting for the punchline. John usually had a funny punchline for his stories. This time, he was silent. I checked my mirrors, allowing my eyes to graze past his face. He looked lost in thought. We continued for a while in silence.

'Then there was the gondola!' he said, an angry tone in his voice.

Again, I turned to look at him sitting in the passenger seat next to me. He was shaking his head. It was like he was talking to himself, trying to make sense of things rather than actually telling me a story.

'My mum and dad had no money. I mean *no* money. Once, this debt collector knocked at the door and Ma opened up her purse and turned it upside down to emphasise it was totally empty. She told him, "You can't get blood out of a stone," then shut the door. Ma would be struggling to make ends meet and Dad would turn up with some useless bit of rubbish he'd bought. One day, instead of bringing his wages home, he arrived with this gaudy plastic gondola. A golden gondola. Seriously! All pleased with himself, he put it on the sideboard and wondered why Ma was so furious. You couldn't make it up. Un-fucking-believable.'

John's candid confession of infidelity set off some difficult encounters between us. If I had too much to drink, I'd get angry and let him have the full wrath of my hurt, which in spite of all the talking still simmered. John insisted he loved me, that he was sorry for the stupid mistakes driven by opportunity, ego, and lust. A bit of fantasy escapism to liven up the ordinary stuff of life. I was hurt but we both agreed we were much better off together, as a team, than we'd be apart.

10

WHO'S IN CHARGE?

By 2005 THINGS settled down and, eventually, looking for the next challenge, I set about creating my own hypnotherapy training course. I based the content on the training I'd received, adding in everything I'd learned from five years in private practice. My course was independently accredited and validated by two of the leading professional bodies.

During the tea break on the first day of that first course, I walked out into the sunshine and called John.

'How's it going?' he asked.

'It's really hard,' I admitted. 'I feel like giving everyone a refund and telling them to go home. What on earth made me think I could do this?'

'Denise,' he said, in his most encouraging tone. 'You *can* do it. It is hard. Remember, if it was easy, anyone could do it. But *they* can't. *You* can.'

After the call with John, on that first day of my first training course, I went back in and finished the day. We never looked back. Soon, I was making enough money that John and I paid off our mortgage. I even bought a sports car, an MG TLF special edition. And John got his Harley Davidson, a teal and cream sportster which roared so loud it made the house shake.

One year when we were on holiday, we decided to have a go at tandem para-gliding. John was in charge, at the back, and was given all the complicated instructions on how to ascend, steer, and descend. I was at the front, having a lovely time, enjoying the experience. I felt safe with John.

Afterwards, he revealed he'd been confused and wasn't at all confident he knew what he was doing. All the time, I'd been blissfully unaware of his insecurity. The trust I had in him to look after me, whatever was happening around us, was total.

Our partnership was a bit like the para-gliding. On the face of it, I looked like the strong one. I was the one at the front. But he was the one behind, pulling the strings, controlling our direction and keeping us safe. I relied on him in so many ways. It was because he provided that rock-solid foundation that I was able to achieve what I did in my career. If he hadn't encouraged, supported, and believed in me, I wouldn't have had sufficient faith in myself to do any of it.

11

WALKING OVER HOT COALS TOGETHER

'YES THAT'S RIGHT.' I held my credit card in one hand and the phone in the other. 'I want a total of five places for the seminar at the Excel Centre in London.' I wondered exactly how a 'free' book ended up costing me nearly £2,000.

When I'd requested the copy of Tony Robbins' book, the person at the other end of the phone enthusiastically persuaded me that not only should I attend the seminar, but my whole family would benefit from going too. To be honest, I didn't need much persuading. I loved such events and was excited at the prospect of sharing the experience with John and our three now adult offspring. That's how all five of us – John and I, Jake, Phoebe, and Liam, all ended up at the Unleash the Power Within three-day event which included a fire walk.

Entering the arena on the first day was in itself a thrilling experience. The atmosphere felt charged. More like a rock concert than a personal development seminar. The pulsating music, the lights, the gigantic video screens showing the action on the stage from every angle. Tony Robbins received a true rock-star reception from the assembled fans and soon to be converts. The can-do attitude and positivity he exuded was contagious. People leapt on their chairs, clapping, singing, and cheering. Robbins, all six-foot-seven of him, handsome and charismatic with exceptionally good teeth, had everyone in the palm of his giant hands.

The big guy boomed at the 10,000-strong crowd:

'Depression is not something you have. It is something you do.'

My stomach lurched. I stopped jumping up and down and cheering my agreement of his every word. I felt as if I was the only one among that crowd who questioned what I'd just heard. Everything else about the event had been amazing. Transformational even. We all threw ourselves enthusiastically into the experience: marching barefoot across red hot coals during the fire walk; laughing and weeping in turn throughout the stream of powerful psychological exercises designed to free us from our most limiting beliefs.

But on this point, I vehemently disagreed with the guru who insisted he was 'noone's guru'. At that moment, I was certain Tony Robbins had got it wrong.

I did not *do* depression.

I *had* depression.

Going back to when I was fourteen, and then more recently, doctors diagnosed me with clinical depression. The 'clinical' preface roots my *depression* firmly in the biomedical realm. That is, relating to biology and medicine. The explanation for which is imbalanced brain chemicals, and the treatment pharmacological. Although the drugs changed from tricyclic when I was fourteen to SSRIs from the 1980s onwards, I believed in the diagnosis. If I am honest, at times the diagnosis provided a certain level of reassurance. It offered a reason for the way I felt. And it promised a solution. The deal was the drugs would correct my faulty biology and all would be well. There wasn't anything I needed to do except, of course, to keep taking the drugs.

'Depression is not something you have. It is something you do.'

12

HAPPY TO BE STUCK WITH YOU

I TRAVELLED to the USA for training that lasted a month and John flew out to stay with me so we could spend time together.

Excitedly, I waited to greet him at the arrivals gate. I'd originally gone to the wrong terminal. But, noticing all the flights on the arrivals board were domestic from within the USA, I ran back to the car park. I drove as fast as I could to the international terminal. I was still in time to see him arrive, looking for me, carrying his bag, and wearing his cream linen Vegas suit like a seasoned traveller.

'Don't talk to me while I'm driving!' I instructed, my white-knuckled hands gripping the steering wheel of my hire car. Although I'd been driving it since I arrived a couple of weeks earlier, I was far from comfortable, concentrating so hard on the road that I missed the sights of the iconic hotels lining the Las Vegas Strip. I still found it crazy that I had taken an eleven hour flight on which I could drink as much alcohol as I wanted, arrived in the USA to an eight hour time difference, and was then handed the keys to a hire car to drive on the wrong side of the road in a foreign country!

John and I spent a week together at a resort in Lake Las Vegas. It was heaven. We visited all the tourist sights. It was August, crazy hot, and we spent hours at the resort pool. As we sat in the shade, sipping our beer straight from the bottle, the wonderfully cheesy song, "Happy to be Stuck with You" by Huey Lewis and the News drifted out from the bar. Life, even with all the ups and downs, seemed quite perfect. And we both agreed: it was the perfect song for us.

One of the colleagues I'd met on the course mentioned how handsome John was and how happy we seemed. *It's true*, I thought. We were more in love and happier than we'd ever been.

When I got back to my room after dropping John back at the airport for his return flight to the UK, I found a note he'd written for me.

I brushed my fingers over the paper, feeling the indents his pen had left behind. Snippets of scenes from our week together flashed through my mind. I couldn't wait for the course to be over so I could get back to the UK. Even though it was only a few hours since he'd gone, I missed him already.

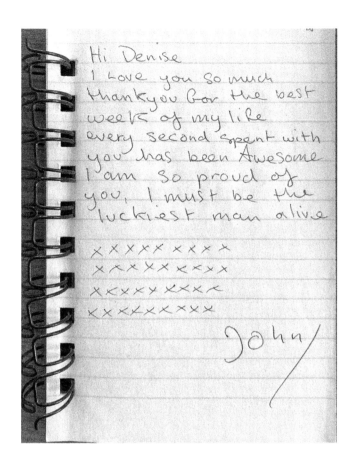

In 2011, I'd donned another mortar board and gown, this time to receive my MSc in coaching from the University of East London. Like my first gradation, John was in the audience. This time accompanied not by my dad, who had sadly passed away, but by Liam. As I walked across the stage to be greeted by the university chancellor I could hear the joyous whoops of congratulations from John and Liam and my heart swelled with pride and happiness. It would be Liam's turn next, an opportunity for John and I as proud parents to see him graduate.

Life was good.

13

COMING HOME

SITTING at the two-seater table in the galley kitchen of our terraced house in Great Baddow, John looked over my shoulder at the screen. He had caught me, yet again, house hunting on Rightmove.com.

John said nothing but I heard him sigh as he walked away. It was always me who brought up the subject of moving house.

It didn't take much to make John happy. He was fine to go with the flow. 'I'm happy if you're happy,' was a mantra of his that sometimes the kids would tease him about. But he genuinely meant it.

The house was fine. It was perfectly serviceable for our requirements. Over the years after buying it, we had adapted and extended it so it wrapped around our needs as a family. A bit like us, it ended up being somewhat unconventional. Everyone who visited would say what a lovely house it was.

Still somehow, it didn't feel like our forever home. So, every couple of years, I'd get itchy feet and start looking. During one of our many house viewings resulting from my periodic searches, John was behaving strangely as the owners showed us around. He seemed distracted and his stance was awkward. I tried my best to act normally and ignore his peculiar antics. I focussed on asking the usual kind of questions and making all the customary comments about what a lovely home they had.

'What the fuck was going on in there?' I hissed once we'd left.

John's characteristic broad grin decorated his face as he pointed down at his shoes. Confused, I looked down. I saw two brown shoes, but there the similarities ended. One was a cotton deck shoe, the other a lace-up trainer with three beige go-faster stripes on each side. I looked at him incredulously.

John rarely, if ever, untied his laces, instead leaving them sufficiently loose to enable him to slip the shoe on. We'd been running late and it wasn't until we were already viewing the house that he looked down and noticed his two odd shoes. By then it was too late.

He shrugged and his grin turned into a belly laugh.

That house viewing had produced a very funny story but otherwise had gotten us precisely nowhere, just like all the others. It was 2012, the kids were grown, and I was on the hunt once again for a new home.

'Come and have a look at this one,' Although a bit further away from our usual search area, 'Rainbow Cottage' met all the requirements. Three bedrooms, detached, a decent-sized garden, a garage that could be used as a workshop, in an area that wasn't too urban and had nice places to walk the dogs.

With a shrug that said *I bet this will come to nothing,* John agreed to go and look. I wasted no time arranging it.

Rainbow Cottage's owners waved us goodbye, their smiles evidence they thought the viewing had gone exceptionally well. John and I walked through the immaculate front garden and back along the unmade road to where we'd parked our car.

'Well?' John said with a smile.

'It is nice,' I paused. 'But it's too small, isn't it?'

Really,

I thought that was going to be John's objection.

He stopped in his tracks, looked me square in the eye and said, 'If we don't buy this place, I never want to hear anything from you about moving house ever again. It's got everything you said you wanted.'

He was right.

It did.

But... it was small.

'Don't you think it's too small?'

'What are you planning to do in there? It's only for the two of us.'

He was right. For the first time in our life together, it would be just the two of us.

We had our share of second thoughts about the move, usually in the morning when we walked the dogs. We'd discuss whether we were doing the right thing, leaving a house that was all right and had been for over two decades, Was it a wise decision to up sticks and move miles away? But by the time evening came we'd both be more relaxed and back on board with the idea.

We wanted to have one last Christmas in the house where our kids had grown up. So we asked our solicitor to stall, holding up the first time purchasers buying our house and the vendors of Rainbow Cottage.

That Christmas was lovely. John and I were centre of the family. We had the older generation, Auntie Olive and my mum, our kids with their respective partners, and our little granddaughter, who delighted in giving out gifts and delighted even more in receiving brightly-wrapped parcels.

The entry in John's diary

On the day of the move, with all the paperwork complete it should have been straight forward. But there was a delay collecting the keys. Feeling a bit tense and confused we sat in the estate agent's office, looking out of the shopfront window at the flakes of falling snow on that chilly January morning. Instead of dropping the keys off, the people moving out of Rainbow Cottage were sitting outside in their car. It was as if, now the day had actually arrived, they didn't want to leave.

The lorry containing everything we owned was also parked outside. The removal guys took the opportunity to have an unexpected break and a smoke. Just another day at work for them.

When we finally got the keys, the process of transporting everything from the lorry into Rainbow Cottage began. My fears about the bijou-snug dimensions were confirmed by the challenge of trying to fit our king sized bed into the tiny bedroom. I glanced at John with an expression that was a mixture of *I told you so* and *oh no* as three removal men struggled with the life-sized jigsaw puzzle.

At that particular moment I was distracted by the lack of a phone signal. Even on this moving day, I had emails to answer. 'Why can't I get a signal?' I said, waving my phone around in the way you do, hoping to locate some magical telecommunication lay-line.

'You're out in the sticks now, love. Have you seen where you've moved?' chipped in one of the removal men as he marched past with a box of stuff.

They were super efficient, and ridiculously quickly it was just the two of us surrounded by boxes. In contrast to all the noise and activity of the actual move, everything now seemed very quiet. Until the doorbell rang.

'Who can that be?' John and I looked at each other, as if by asking the question we would acquire a supernatural predictive gift of seeing through walls and doors.

It was Joyce, our new neighbour from across the road, who took the time to come and welcome us to the neighbourhood. I will never forget how much that simple act of kindness meant to us at a time when we wondered if we'd done the right thing.

Only some of the boxes were labelled with the name of the room they should go to, so it was a bit of a lucky dip every time we opened one. But by that evening, miraculously, we were pretty much unpacked. We sat down to a steak dinner, which I managed to cook on an unfamiliar stove, accompanied by the usual bottle of red.

We chinked glasses, sharing our customary toast, 'Chin-chin. Here's to us and a new phase in our life together.'

Taking a sip of the smooth warm wine, I glanced around the cosy kitchen and then looked across the table at John.

'It feels like we've come home.'

In December 2015, John and I decided to stop drinking. Phoebe had come to live with us after the breakup of a relationship and she was teetotal, which made us think. When it had been just the two of us, our nightly tipple was our business. We loved indulging in our red wine ritual but, in truth, we both knew that perhaps we were drinking a bit too much than was healthy.

'I blame the supermarket,' John once said, only half joking. 'Those special offers of three bottles of Dreamtime Ridge for the price of two are just too good to pass up!'

Auntie Olive's husband, Alb, who became disabled soon after they married, had once told her, 'Don't ever drink because you're stressed and think you need it. Only have a drink as a treat. Enjoy and savour it.' So at noon every day (not a minute earlier) Auntie Olive would have a brandy and ginger. She might have another later in the evening, but at noon she'd only have the one.

Auntie Olive had the right idea. She experienced a lot of stress in her life but always remained one of the most positive, upbeat, and optimistic people I have ever known. Her mantra was, 'I am confident, competent, cheerful, and calm.'

My Auntie Olive and Uncle Alb

Reactions to us not drinking were fascinating. My sister said she'd never have another night out with me because I would be 'no fun'. Others couldn't understand how we enjoyed a celebration, or indulged in a commiseration, or anything in between, without alcohol.

'What? You don't drink *at all*? Not *ever*?'

Tired of trying to explain our decision, in the face of yet another plea to, "Go on – just have one," I started telling people we were raging alcoholics. 'Do you really want to be responsible for us falling off the wagon?' I'd say.

Sometimes John would tell me off for using the 'raging alcoholic' line, but it usually did the trick. People would shift about, fidget, avoid eye contact, mutter apologies, and quickly change the topic of conversation. Once safely out of earshot, John and I would howl with laughter at their reactions.

As a result of cutting out the booze, I lost loads of weight and John said he felt healthier than he had done in years.

I was still dutifully taking the antidepressants. After all the doctor had told me my condition – my depression was the result of a chemical imbalance in the brain. Because he'd never said, and I never thought to ask how the chemicals might get re-balanced, the assumption was I would be on the medication for life.

In general, life has more *ands* than *ors*. That is – life is happy *and* sad, good *and* bad, joyful *and* depressing, scary *and* exciting. We had plenty of ups and downs but on balance more was right in our world than wrong.

One of the downs was the end of Jake's marriage to Louise, when their two children were still really little. On the upside, however, it meant we saw a lot more of Jake and our grandchildren. We loved the sleepovers and playing in the garden on the trampoline or in the sandpit. John built them a treehouse, and a rope swing hung from the apple tree. We made cakes, painted, played games, sang and danced and watched their favourite movies on a loop. We took them on holiday too: Peppa Pig World and Butlin's.

There were toddler swimming lessons, which Ruby excelled at but Josh found a bit overwhelming. And trips to the park, the beach, and the zoo.

I took them for their first ever cinema outing. Ruby loved it but Josh found it all a bit overwhelming – a bit of a theme when they were small. Although there is only fifteen months' difference in age, even as toddlers Ruby was definitely the big sister, often found cooing over the cuteness of her little brother.

During one trip to the Sea Life centre when Ruby was about three and Josh two, she stepped in when Josh was asked a question. 'Josh don't talk,' she said as if letting her brother off the hook in an interrogation. That became a bit of a catch phrase for us whenever Ruby took over.

John would get a bit irritated with me for the financial support I provided to Jake. He rightly thought Jake should be making more of an effort to find work. But I figured we were at a stage in our lives where we could afford to help. John and I did not live an extravagant lifestyle. Plus I could still vividly remember how awful it was to be a single parent short of money.

Our first Christmas at Rainbow Cottage, the front garden resembled the entrance to Santa's grotto. Like my father, John went overboard on the decorations. There was an assortment of oversized inflatables: a snowman in a top hat; 6ft high gift boxes; and a Santa on a motorcycle, somewhat strangely pulled by reindeer.

One evening in 2016, John and I were at home watching TV when we got a call from Jake. He said Auntie Olive had called him because she was feeling unwell. He was about to go on stage in some 'Am dram' show; the children were with their mum.

For the previous couple of months, at my request, Jake had been taking Olive shopping once a week. He lived only a few minutes away from her and had time because he didn't have a job. Olive had loaned him the money for a car and I was paying her back monthly on his behalf.

As soon as Jake hung up, I called Olive. She sounded very poorly but managed to tell me an ambulance was on its way.

'John and I are leaving right now. We'll be there soon.'

I put my foot down and we did the journey from our home to Olive's in record time. When we got there, Olive was already in the back of the ambulance, drifting in and out of consciousness.

'We're going to blue light her to Broomfield hospital. Don't try to keep up with us,' the paramedic informed me. John jumped into the ambulance and I followed behind.

At the hospital we were shown to a relatives' room and started making calls.

I called Phoebe. 'Will you pop over to let Grandma know, please?'

The relationship between my mum and Olive had been strained since the death of my dad, so Mum considered it a betrayal that I remained close to Olive.

'Of course. And I'll stay with her until we know what's going on.'

John called Liam and my sister. Jake wasn't answering his phone so I guessed he must be on stage.

Eventually the door opened and a doctor entered. In a sombre tone he explained Olive had suffered heart failure.

'She was resuscitated and we managed to get a heartbeat, but it's unsustainable and she's in the process of actively dying. Would you like to be with her?'

Olive lay motionless, eyes closed. Each laboured breath filled the room with a chesty rattling sound. I stroked her hair and told her how much she was loved and what an absolute honour it was to be her niece. Minutes later, everything went quiet and she died.

After another brief spell in the relatives' room, we were given her belongings in a plastic supermarket carrier bag. Olive would not have been impressed. We made our way in silence through the darkness to the car park. My phone rang. It was Jake.

'She's gone,' I told him. He started to cry and said how guilty he felt. I thought he meant about his choice to go on stage. I reassured him how much Auntie Olive loved him and that none of us could have predicted her death.

John and I decided it best to leave collecting Olive's dog until the next day. The prospect of introducing a newcomer to our pack was a bit daunting. When we let ourselves into Olive's neat and tidy terraced house, it felt lifeless. As always, it was immaculate except for the tell-tale signs the paramedics had been there; discarded stickers from the ECG lay on the floor of the lounge together with some packaging, I guess from medication.

Olive's address book was on the table alongside a letter from her GP. I called the surgery. Then I called the ophthalmic department of the hospital to cancel her up-coming appointment. For the past year I'd been taking her for the regular injections required to keep the macular degeneration at bay. I glanced at the back of the address book, I read the words written in her swirly handwriting: *Where a pessimist sees problems in every situation, an optimist sees opportunity.*

Olive was a very organised woman. She had been a secretary when it was a truly professional position. Long before the days of computers, the role required considerable brain power. She'd always kept a ledger along with receipts, diligently tracking her income and expenditure. Since retirement this activity was more for enjoyment than necessity. Of late she'd been getting a bit confused and forgetful, and she'd stopped bothering with 'doing her accounts'. We'd discussed whether she might feel less isolated in supported living. I even took her to view a couple of flats with emergency pull cords and wardens. In all honesty I think she regarded these as enjoyable excursions rather than a serious search for a new home. It was no surprise she decided to stay put. She loved her little house.

Following Olive's death certain things surfaced resulting in family estrangement. I'm not sure if my 'depression' got worse or if I was just reacting normally to what was a depressing situation. John displayed his usual stoic attitude.

'It is what it is. We can only focus on the things we can influence. There's no point wasting energy on things we can't control, like what others say or do.'

His words reminded me of that day all those years before in the rowing boat, on the lake, in the park.

It is a universal truth that the only constant in life is change. Nothing remains the same. Sometimes the changes are obvious and pivotal – a birth, a death, a significant beginning, or a definitive end. And sometimes life just evolves. Like the hole created in the rock at St Nectan's Glen. A constant flow of water over an extended period of time, shaped that landscape. The change was not made from one explosion, but gradually; a day at a time, a drop at a time. Olive used to say, 'Nothing lasts – not the good and not the bad. So during the good take time to fully enjoy it. And during the bad, remember, this too shall pass.'

14

TIME TICKS AWAY

JANUARY 2017

TWENTY-ONE MONTHS BEFORE DAY ZERO

THE INITIAL WEIGHT loss I enjoyed as a result of giving up wine had plateaued and Phoebe was also heavier than she wanted to be. So we thought a week of juices and soups would be a good kick start to the New Year. John stayed home with the dogs while Phoebe and I attended a health retreat. There was plenty to keep our minds off our empty stomachs; various fitness classes, a gym, long hikes in the woods and yoga. Lots of yoga.

The yoga studio was breathtaking. A perfect setting. It featured an entire wall of glass which created an ever-changing spectacular natural artwork of sky, trees, and mountains. The colours shifted and switched depending on the time of day and changing light.

As the class progressed, the room was bathed in a serene dark orange glow of sunset. Carefully arranged tea light candles delicately illuminated the space with their flickering dance. Streams of curling smoke from burning incense filled the air with a musky fragrance. The class concluded and we prepared for meditation. The mat beneath me felt as if it were somehow flying. Soft yet enveloping, like the comforting darkness that wrapped me in a sense of safety, security, and pure love.

My mind wandered, considering all those who had come and gone during the time John and I had been together. People made their entrances and exits like bit part players to our leading characters. Most significantly, John and I always had one another.

The combination of the melodic tone of the teacher's voice gently guiding the meditation and the accompanying music had an ethereal power that seemed to transport me somewhere else, beyond this dimension.

I felt John's hand in mine, even though he was miles away back home in the UK. It felt so real, as if we were actually together, holding hands, sharing the experience. I found myself smiling, my heart and soul overwhelmed by love, safe in the knowledge John would be there to greet me on my return.

15

COFFEE AND YOGA
TWELVE MONTHS BEFORE DAY ZERO

I GOT an email informing me that Kenny, the yoga teacher who had been such a special part of the juice retreat experience, was leading another, again in Portugal, this time in Monchique.

'Are you up for it?' I asked John.

'I can't even touch my toes.' John leaped to his feet to demonstrate his lack of flexibility. 'But if you think I'll be okay, then yes. Why not?'

'You will love it.' I said with absolute certainty.

I was right.

We shared a truly fabulous week. In addition to the twice daily yoga, there was a beautiful spa, meditation under the full moon, trekking through woods and up mountains. We located a natural spring and filled our water bottles from it. The whole group really hit it off so in the evenings after dinner we'd go to the bar, sing songs and tell stories. And we laughed. A lot. That's where John and I sat in the café in the square, sipping espressos, happily enjoying a spot of people watching.

John and I on a hike in Monchique

16

JOHN GETS INTO TROUBLE!
EIGHT MONTHS BEFORE DAY ZERO

'I GOT STOPPED BY THE POLICE,' John said, the corners of his eyes crinkling just like they always did when he's having a bit of fun.

George, our host, looked genuinely concerned. 'The police?'

It was February, 2018, and I was in Istanbul on a business trip, teaching a course. A few years prior, I had run training for the same organisation but I had missed John so much that when they invited me back, I insisted I'd only go if he could accompany me.

We both loved Istanbul. The first night, George had taken us out for dinner for a traditional Turkish meal: kofte; kuzu tandir; döner; and lahmacun. There was music and entertainment. I was surprised the belly dancers were all male but George explained it was tradition dating back to the Ottoman Empire when women were largely prohibited from performing on stage.

After dinner we drank thick strong coffee served in tiny cups called *fincan*. The walls of the restaurant displayed photographs of all their celebrity customers. John and I had no idea who most of them were. It was a brilliant night.

The next day, just before I was about to begin the class, John popped into the conference room. In a low whisper, he told me he was about to do some exploring. I gave him a quick peck on the cheek and returned to my place at the front of the room.

'It is so sweet,' one of the students remarked, 'how your face lights up when your husband enters the room.' The students – most of them local business people – were attentive, diligent, and enthusiastic. Since my previous visit to Turkey, I noticed the atmosphere in Istanbul had shifted. It wasn't as carefree and friendly as it had been before.

John explained to George and I that he'd walked across the bridge that separates the European from the Asian part of Istanbul. He watched people fish from the bridge and ventured into the Anatolian side of the city.

'There was a demonstration. The police had guns and there was a water cannon. I took some photos on my phone. The police asked me who I was and what I was doing. They insisted I delete the photos.'

George's expression became even more intense.

'You were fortunate they spoke English to you. The last foreign tutor we had here got himself arrested and it took us two days just to locate where he was being held!'

John and I exchanged a glance.

'Best not do anything like that again,' George concluded.

I could tell from John's smile he was already planning his next expedition.

John was irrepressible, impulsive, and quite fearless.

Little did I know when John left this for me on 14th February 2018 that it was the last ever Valentine's card he would give me.

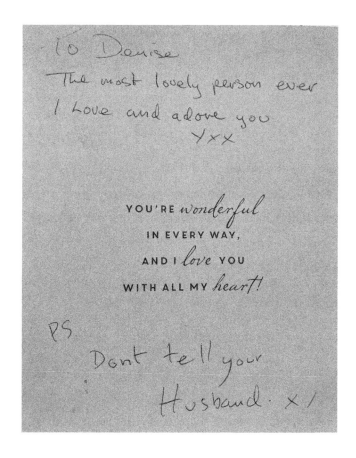

17

JOHN'S 60TH BIRTHDAY

SIX MONTHS BEFORE DAY ZERO

FIRST THING on the morning of 13th April 2018, John went off to start his 60th birthday with a massage. When he returned, suitably chilled out, I prepared a full English breakfast: sausages; bacon; mushrooms; fried eggs; baked beans; hot buttered toast; and tea. John, Phoebe, and I sat together at the kitchen table to eat.

As he was about to open his gifts, his phone rang.

'Leave it,' I said, 'it's your birthday. You've got the day off.'

'But it might be one of those have-you-had-an-accident ambulance-chaser-type calls,' he said, a glint in his eye. Now, this might seem odd but John loved these calls. While most of us get irritated by them, far from being annoyed at the interruption, John relished the opportunity to have a laugh.

Phoebe and I exchanged a smile and she got out her phone, ready to record John's response as he answered the call. That way we could enjoy it again on demand.

During one such unsolicited call, the replay of which we'd watched many times, John exclaimed how remarkable it was that they knew to call him! And, yes! He *had* been in an accident that wasn't his fault! He started off by giving sensible responses to their questions. But this soon descended into the most outlandish and elaborate story. He explained how he'd been rear-ended by a car driven by a senior member of the royal family, which resulted in him getting a gear stick stuck in an unspeakable place. John went into detail about how the medics at the hospital A & E department had sadly failed to remove it, so there it remained, even as they spoke.

The call on John's birthday morning sadly turned out only to be a potential customer wanting to book an estimate. After John had finished agreeing a date and writing it in his diary, Phoebe and I continued to tease him about him being a year closer to his retirement pension.

We gave him his assorted gifts. Silly 'You are sixty' type things. A mug that said *British 1958 Classic*, a key ring with coins minted the year he was born, a sign that read *If you haven't grown up by the time you're sixty, you don't have to*, a t-shirt emblazoned with *Vintage superior goods 1958 premium product*. Just simple tokens to celebrate his reaching a milestone birthday.

Later we drove to nearby Cressing Temple Barns, where we met Liam for afternoon tea. It was a lovely day. We laughed and joked, enjoyed each others' company, and took daft photos. Among the silly snaps we took is one that is quite lovely – of John in chain mail wielding a sword.

On the surface, it's just typical John playing around, dressed up and posing. But in the instant I hit the button to take the photo, I captured something. There is a seriousness to his expression, to his pose. He holds the sword in both hands, his wedding ring clearly visible, the blade resting against his left shoulder as if ready to strike some adversary. The image conveys something John didn't often show the world; a depth to his character. That expression, a slight frown, the angle of his head, his eyes looking directly into the lens. Unflinching, an expression of strength and power across his face. With his bushy white beard and short hair, he could have been a medieval knight. The natural light in that place produced a beautiful sepia hue, no filter required. The image captured forever an otherwise fleeting moment.

18

A WEDDING, A HOSPITAL AND THE HOLIDAY INN

FIVE MONTHS BEFORE DAY ZERO

I WOKE with a jolt to the sound of John retching in the hotel bathroom.

'It's indigestion from the pizza. Or drinking too much coffee too late. I'll have a shower and I'll be fine,' John said, but he hadn't convinced me.

We were on the beautiful and picturesque Greek island of Santorini for Liam's wedding to Claudia – an event two years in the planning.

Claudia, a project manager by profession, had meticulously organised every last detail from the perfect flowers to the harpist. It was the night before the nuptials and we had not long returned from drinks with the family in the bar, perched atop a cliff, looking down on whitewashed houses, blue-domed churches, and beautiful, dramatic views of the ocean. A scene of picture-postcard prettiness. We had watched the sun slowly set, a magnificent display of yellow and deep orange. On our way back to the hotel, we ate ice cream and I bought Claudia a little infinity charm for good luck.

With John being sick again, I rang reception.

'There's no point calling a doctor. Best you go straight to the clinic,' said the guy on night duty reception. 'I'll organise a taxi.'

Leaning on Phoebe for support, John made his way to the waiting car while I tossed a few things into a bag.

John's face was grey. I was scared. The taxi driver, who didn't speak much English, wore an expression of concern as he helped John inside the newly built and brightly-lit clinic and shouted to summon help.

Over the next few hours, John drifted in and out of a drug-fuelled sleep, attached by wires to beeping monitors. John's complexion was still waxy, his expression pained, and it seemed to me his condition was deteriorating.

The staff at the clinic were efficient and thorough but noone was telling me what was happening. Partly, at least, because of the language barrier.

I watched, feeling helpless, as two doctors staring at an X-ray seemed to be arguing. I couldn't understand their words, but soon learned they disagreed over whether John had a pulmonary embolism, in which case it would be too dangerous for him to fly, or a cardiac problem, in which case he needed to be flown, without delay, from the island clinic to a hospital on the mainland. In either case, if they were wrong it could kill him.

I agonised over whether to call Liam and Claudia and disturb them just before the wedding. Part of me hoped John would make a miraculous recovery and that, in just a few hours, we'd make the wedding with a story to tell. I imagined I might yet get to wear the big purple hat which had caused such a fuss as hand luggage on the plane and that John would get to wear the lovely suit he looked so handsome in. He didn't get the chance to dress up very often and was pleased with himself in it.

I kept in touch with Phoebe by WhatsApp. *I've told Claudia's family Dad is in the hospital and that you are with him*, I read in one of her messages. But she hadn't yet informed Liam and Claudia.

Early in the morning, I messaged Ally, Claudia's mum, asking what she thought I should do. She suggested I tell them and give them the opportunity to see John before the wedding, especially as noone knew yet what was wrong with him.

Liam and Claudia arrived at the hospital and spent some time with us. John was pretty much out of it but I appreciated them being there.

Plans progressed to transfer John to a hospital on the mainland. Liam drove like a maniac across the island to our hotel to collect our passports and grab a few more things we'd need. With a quick, tear-stained kiss, he raced off again, this time to get married. Without his mum or dad there to witness it.

An ambulance whisked us through dark, unfamiliar streets and through tall wire gates to a waiting area near a runway at the airport. Armed guards patted me down and checked our passports, a stark contrast to our experience on arriving on Santorini, and we waited for the military plane that would transport us off the island.

Amidst and in spite of all the mayhem – the deafening roar of plane engines, the beeping of reversing vehicles and their yellow flashing lights, the rough texture of the hospital blanket, the unfamiliar medical smells – everything seemed to go strangely still and quiet. I rested my forehead on John's arm. Half to myself, half out loud, I whispered, 'Is there anything we need to talk about?'

Suddenly John seemed conscious and aware. 'I'm not going to die, am I?' He grabbed my arm and tried to pull himself up. I lifted my head and met his eyes, which seemed to telegraph to me his strong will to live. I was desperately worried about him but I knew I had to keep it together for John. He was the sick one. I wanted to be strong for him. As confidently as I could, I reassured him, and he was calm again.

Paramedics threw open the rear doors of the ambulance and wheeled John and his stretcher out. 'Keep your head down and run in the middle up the ramp and into the plane,' the soldier shouted to me over the roar of the engines, while pointing into the belly of the large military aircraft.

The flight was turbulent. Hung from the ceiling on his stretcher, John swung back and forth so madly that the cannula in his arm dislodged. I looked over to see the white sheet covering him turn crimson. I thought he was dead.

It was still dark when we landed. 'Where are we? What country?' The paramedic with us in the back of another ambulance looked at me like I was a crazy lady. 'Greece. Athens.'

The mainland hospital was rundown and dirty, the corridors piled high with junk. The facilities were dismal. I tried to call Liam but was sent to his voicemail. 'Can you get us out of here? If what Dad has wrong with him doesn't kill him, whatever he catches in this place will!'

The facilities were awful so I washed John with antibacterial wipes. I went out each day to buy food from local shops and brought it back to him. At night I slept in a chair by his bedside. I was not about to leave him there alone and vulnerable.

After several days, John was considered fit to fly and we staged our escape. Liam came through and booked us onto the first available flight, which wasn't until the next day. We grabbed a taxi to the airport and booked into an adjacent hotel.

After the hospital, the Holiday Inn felt like five-star luxury. The powerful jet of hot water in the first shower since leaving Santorini felt heavenly, the basic complimentary shower gel and shampoo smelled like a spa treatment. We ate chicken salad in the small hotel restaurant. Still famished a couple of hours later, we ordered another meal through room service. The simple food seemed amazing.

During all our years together, John and I had stayed in some pretty incredible places. But sleeping together in a bed with clean sheets, knowing that we would be on a flight home the next day, that night in the airport Holiday Inn was something very special.

Although we missed their big fancy wedding in Santorini, John and I had at least been at Liam and Claudia's official marriage which took place on 2nd May. They married in the same register office in Camberwell Southwark where we'd married three decades before. We couldn't be certain, but John thought it was actually the very same room.

19

WE COULD LIVE HERE

FOUR MONTHS BEFORE DAY ZERO

I WAS TOYING with the idea of extending my business by offering personal development retreats. I'd successfully hosted a couple in the UK but decided it would be nice to hold a few somewhere the sun was guaranteed. I swivelled the screen of my laptop so John could see the place I had found. He leaned in, reading the description of the resort in Dalyan, Turkey; a peaceful setting among orange and pomegranate trees in the shadow of beautiful mountains. He studied the photos.

'Looks amazing,' he said.

'Shall we go and do a recce?' I asked. 'Let's face it, we could do with a break. Santorini wasn't exactly relaxing.'

'Well, I suppose you would have to check it out personally before you decide it's the right venue for a retreat,' he smiled.

So on 11th of June, 2018, we were back on an international flight, this time to Dalyan, Turkey.

It was dark when we landed so we went straight to bed. Stepping out onto the balcony in the morning and taking in for real the views we had seen on the website was as close to love at first sight as you can get. The entire place turned out to be just what I'd hoped; a family run resort brimming with genuine friendly warmth. John loved Sooty, the resort dog, who happily howled her accompaniment to every call to prayer, broadcast from the nearby mosques.

We spent a chilled out week making plans and enjoying ourselves. John lounged by the pool and I claimed the treehouse as my place of work. We did all the tourist trips: Istuzu beach; the mud baths; the ancient ruins. We visited the rescue centre for street dogs. We were inspired by the adventurous true story of 'Kaptan June' who stopped hotel developers from building on the saved the beach where the loggerhead turtles lay their eggs.

'Only one in one thousand of the hatchlings make it to adulthood,' the guide told us as we watched tiny turtles swim in the tanks at the conservation centre.

'Wow. That's a powerful statistic about beating overwhelming odds,' I said.

One evening after dinner, we sat contentedly watching the swallows dip and dive at twilight. John stretched and sighed, 'I could quite happily live here.'

I smiled broadly. I'd been thinking exactly the same. Out came the phones and we both started searching properties on rightmove.com. Taking it in turns, we read out descriptions and revealed photos, followed by exclamations of, 'Guess how much?'

It seemed as if we could swap Rainbow Cottage for a pretty grand home here. People do that kind of thing: go away on holiday, fall in love with the place, and think about how great it would be to move. But we were serious. We discussed the possibilities of life in a warm climate, offering a more slow and simple pace. I could continue my private practice, seeing individual clients via video call, potentially even running training courses using the same medium. Or perhaps it was feasible to return to the UK to run face-to-face courses while we focussed our marketing efforts on building the retreat business.

'I could do all the airport transfers and be a tour guide on the day trips for our retreat guests,' John said. 'I'd ensure everything ran smoothly.'

I nodded. I could envision it. 'If we eventually buy somewhere big enough to host the retreats, you could do the cooking.' John loved cooking. His tastes in food were much more adventurous than mine.

We continued the discussion the next day, standing waist high in the clear blue ocean, gently rocked by the motion of the waves, the feeling of the sand beneath our feet. We had options, possibilities, choices. We owned Rainbow Cottage outright, having worked hard to completely pay off another mortgage.

Gazing out at the blue-on-blue horizon of sea and sky, we discussed how much better off we were than others we knew who had well paid jobs but also had lots of debt.

Via the power of Facebook, we contacted some other English people who had made the move. They told us about their day-to-day lives and how much they loved it. They told us to just do it!

I glanced over at John to see him looking at me with that cheeky *well, shall we?* expression.

As soon as we returned to the UK, we organised a second trip the following month. Primarily to make arrangements for our first retreat, planned for October 2018, and also to further explore our potential relocation.

John was prepared to up sticks and just go but I favoured more caution. I wanted to keep our options open to see if there was a way to make the move and keep our home in the UK. I had a few concerns about the political situation in Turkey. There was a growing shift towards more strict adherence to Islam and I wondered if that might mean a less tolerant attitude to foreigners in the future?

While John and I were united in our desire to move to Dalyan, I was reluctant to burn bridges and do anything that meant we might find ourselves in a situation we couldn't come back from.

20

A CALL NO ONE IS EVER READY FOR
FIFTEEN DAYS BEFORE DAY ZERO

A call no one is ever ready for

THE SMILE on John's face melted, drawing all his features downward where they became rigid and pained. It was John's twin brother Jim on the phone with bad news. We were sitting at the table having just finished our Sunday lunch – my signature slow-roasted pulled pork, fluffy potatoes, and steamed vegetables.

We all fell silent, watching John as he listened to Jim. Ruby and Josh stared at their grandpa, sensing something awful was happening but not quite understanding what.

'Come on kids,' Claudia said brightly, 'let's go in the living room.' She ushered them away to play.

'I'm okay, but the thing is...' I could hear Jim's voice through the phone. 'It's now gone to stage four, so they're saying months or maybe weeks.'

Years before, Jim had made a full recovery after testicular cancer. But this time this cancer was more aggressive and, despite treatment, it seemed Jim would not beat the odds.

What had been a pleasant yet uneventful family day became the starting point for a series of events that would end in tragedy.

The twins, John and Jim, were two of seven children. John told me that before they moved to their house in Bermondsey when he was eleven, the family had lived in cramped, rented accommodation with shared facilities. He told of having gas lamps long after most homes had electric lighting. He told me they had a coin-operated TV that would shut off half-way through programmes when the money ran out. I was never sure if he was winding me up or if these stories were true.

John's mum only ever spoke of the good times. She was a quiet, strong, Irish Catholic woman who always ensured her children were immaculately dressed for church and other outings.

'Are all these children yours?' people would ask. Proudly, she would say, 'They are!'

John described a childhood where things were often not explained. A bus would turn up and the twins would be put on it. Off to a new school? Off to a summer camp run by nuns? John said noone ever told them in advance where they were going or what was going to happen.

Jim grew up to be a deep thinker with a wealth of general knowledge and a cheeky sense of fun. He was quite a character but never married or had children of his own. In all the time I knew him, I never heard him say a bad word about anyone. John was always a little bit more confident and outgoing than Jim, but just as thoughtful and kind.

As adults, the twins didn't see each other frequently. Jim used to joke, 'Once Denise came along, that was it. I was replaced.' But nevertheless, they were twins and retained a special bond.

John and I didn't speak directly about Jim's cancer for the rest of the day. We carried on as if nothing had happened. Visits with the grandchildren were rare these days and I cherished the time I got to spend with them. Selfishly, I didn't want anything to spoil that precious day.

John's expression was vacant when he finally joined the rest of us in the living room. He sat on the sofa facing Ruby, who was in full performance mode playing one of her favourite games. She was the teacher, relegating the rest of us to roles as her students. Like any real classroom, there's always at least one kid not paying attention.

'Grandpa, you're not listening!' Ruby was used to John playing the naughty schoolboy. Much to Josh's amusement and Ruby's indignation, John would find increasingly creative ways to misbehave and challenge the authority of the teacher.

John's playful nature was apparent not just in his ability to immerse himself in the grandchildren's games; he joyfully animated so many of our shared experiences.

For example, a few years before, I was exhibiting at a mind, body, and spirit festival with a view to attracting new clients and students. John came along to help me set up and to provide me with a bit of moral support. As he was classified as an exhibitor too, John got free entry to all the workshops on offer. So while I manned the stand, John informed me he was going to a shamanic workshop to discover what his spirit animal was. After quite a short time he came back.

'What happened? Didn't you like it?' I asked.

'Not at all. I was really enjoying myself. Got right into it. But I got asked to leave.' I recognised that all too familiar glint of mischief in his eye.

'Why?' I asked. 'What did you do?'

'Well, the workshop leader started off by banging a drum and getting us to meditate. She described how we should imagine we were flying over mountain tops and running through valleys, until we got to a lake. She said we should look in the still water of the lake and whatever we saw reflected there, that is our spirit animal.' His grin was wide and I could see how much he was enjoying recounting the adventure. 'Everyone else saw majestic creatures like wolves and eagles. I just told her what I saw,' he paused, drawing out the suspense.

'And what did you see?'

'It was a bright pink My Little Pony with a rainbow mane.' His laughter now spilling over and filling the space between us. He kept trying to finish the story but had to keep stopping to wipe his eyes as he tried to contain his giggling.

'I swear, it was just like the My Little Pony that Phoebe had when she was little!' His giggling was infectious and now I was laughing too.

'The workshop leader accused me of not taking the exercise seriously and told me to leave.'

John could effortlessly make up imaginative games to play with our grandchildren that were hilarious to witness.

In one such game, Ruby and Josh would set up shops, their stock comprised of items collected from around our house and displayed on our nest of tables from the living room.

John would play the part of Challenging Customer. At first, he'd enter the shop merely browsing for nothing in particular. This would quickly turn to him enquiring if they had more and more outlandish items. The kids would giggle uncontrollably, attempting but failing to remain in character as the shopkeepers. They'd assure him they could get the item and instruct him to return at a set time. Then Ruby and Josh would scurry around the house looking for whatever it was.

John would return and they'd proudly produce the thing he'd asked for, at which point John would change his mind and come up with absurd reasons the item was not quite what he wanted. Or he'd haggle about price because of defects he'd spotted. I'd watch, astounded at his creative imagination and immense patience, both amused and touched by his ability to so effortlessly entertain.

After the call from Jim, John wasn't playful. He looked worried and lost in his thoughts.

'John!' I nodded in the direction of Ruby.

He snapped out of it and did a passable job of engaging in Ruby's game but it was easy for me to see his smile was forced; his mind was clearly still somewhere else entirely.

That evening, once John and I were alone again, we focussed on the practicalities of him going to London to see his family. We talked about train times and rearranging work. Beyond that, we carried on as if everything were normal. It was an odd juxtaposition because on one hand the news about Jim meant everything had changed but on the other, in our world in that moment, everything appeared the same.

We sat in front of the TV, tuning in to a horror series we'd been happily binge watching on Netflix. With a growing sense of unease, the themes of death and ghosts and what funeral directors do to corpses took on an altogether darker meaning.

21

THE FINAL FOURTEEN DAYS

15TH OCTOBER

THE NEXT MORNING John took the train to London. He went to his mum's house, caught up with his siblings, and accompanied Jim to a hospital appointment. Although his cancer was advanced, Jim was still in good spirits and for all intents and purposes appeared reasonably fit and well.

The two of them had lunch at Jim's favourite pub. They talked of going to Egypt together, reminiscing about their long ago adventure to the Middle East. Jim had 'done India' and been to many places but a trip to see the pyramids and to sail along the Nile had long been on his bucket list, and it was literally a case of now or never.

I doubt either of them really believed that any doctor would sanction such a trip but they played along with the idea as it was still a possibility.

John stayed overnight at Liam and Claudia's. The next day we exchanged texts.

If you want to stay to spend more time with Jim - it's fine with me.

To which John replied, *No I need to get back home. I'm missing you way too much.*

There's no quick fix to emotional pain, shock, or anticipatory grief. But I encouraged John to make an appointment with the GP. I'd been on antidepressants for years so while I knew they weren't 'happy pills', I hoped the doctor might give John something to take the edge off and help him sleep.

Following John's visit to see Jim, we did our weekly shop at the local supermarket. While loading bags into the boot of the car it was obvious to me that John's characteristic optimism was nowhere to be seen. He seemed on edge and agitated. I decided to address one of the issues I guessed might be on his mind.

'What's going to happen to Dave and your mum when Jim goes?'

Their mum was getting on in years and Dave has special needs. Jim had become the main carer for Dave following the death of their father. The three of them made an odd little family unit but it worked and they got on really well.

John slammed the boot shut. 'Jim isn't dead yet!' he snapped.

In the thirty-three years we'd known each other, John had only ever snapped at me a few times.

'I know. I'm sorry. I was just...'

I was always 'just'.

Just trying to think of answers to questions which hadn't been asked or *just* trying to find solutions to problems we did not have. I was the depressive one. Always thinking ahead, usually to the worst possible outcome.

'I'm sorry.' I repeated.

'Me too.' He sighed.

I had known Jim almost as long as I'd known John but it was obvious that however sad I was feeling, John must be feeling so much worse. Jim was his brother – his *twin* brother.

On 19th October, Liam and Claudia brought Jim up from London to visit us. Jim was his usual upbeat and optimistic self. We went out for dinner. John seemed nervous, distracted. He got really annoyed with himself about parking. I thought he was acting out of character but assumed it was all a reaction to the news about Jim. I had no reason to consider that it might be anything else.

The week of 22nd to 26th October I was due to be away. I felt torn. I did not want to leave John but the reason for the trip was to help support Liam who was trying to get his own coaching business off the ground.

Liam needed my help as he wasn't a certified NLP (Neuro Linguistic Programming) trainer and I was. The course had been arranged for a while. I told myself I had to fulfil the commitment. At least John wouldn't be by himself; Phoebe was home. They got on well. They liked the same kind of music and TV programmes. They enjoyed each other's company.

The course was full on and actually gave me something to focus on, rather than thinking about what was going on in our family. That time away provided a little emotional respite, a few days to gather myself so I could be supportive and helpful to John on my return. Liam and I took the opportunity to meet up with Jim a couple of times during that week.

John was waiting for me at the station when I arrived home on the Friday evening. I have no idea how, but he managed to place himself in exactly the right position on the platform so that when the doors opened, he was right there – the first thing I saw.

It was good to be home. We had faced tough times before and we would do what we always did: get through whatever was to come *together* as a team.

John didn't sleep well that night. Next morning he got up early and seemed jumpy. I drove him to Kelvedon station where he caught the train, yet again to London. Understandably, he wanted to be there for Jim who had another hospital appointment.

During the day we exchanged upbeat messages. John remarked on how fit Jim seemed – how far they had walked and what they were eating. He didn't stay in London overnight but came home as the grandchildren were visiting us the following day.

22

THE DAY BEFORE THE DAY THE WORLD ENDED

28TH OCTOBER 2018

BEFORE THEY ARRIVED, John went to the shop to buy Ruby and Josh small gifts so we could play a game of hot and cold treasure hunt. Predictably, the day involved a game of schools where Ruby was teacher. We had to double up on our acting roles as, in a twist to the usual game, Ruby decided we should be not only the pupils but also the parents attending parents' evening too.

Although it was a fun filled day, John did not seem himself. He kept getting up and walking from room to room as if unable to settle.

'You okay?'

Ruby and I were at the kitchen table making school work assignments. John had been in the living room playing Harry Potter with Josh

'Yes, yes. Just thought I'd come and see what you're up to?'

At the end of the visit, while getting the kids in the car to take them home, I offered to drive, joking with John,

'I'll be pilot, and you can be chief entertainment officer.'

'Aren't I always?' He smiled.

23

DAY ZERO

'WHO CAN WE CALL?' one of the officers asked.

I gazed at them but didn't really see them. I looked at their uniforms. Their muddy boots. Their empathetic expressions. It crossed my mind that they'd likely recount this whole interaction as a guess-what-I-did-at-work-today type of conversation. Perhaps one would describe the scene to a partner over dinner or maybe to friends in the pub. People would shake their heads and say, 'How sad.'

Was this really happening?

As a therapist, I'd heard many clients use the expression *numb with shock*. Having some intellectual comprehension of what it means is one thing. The physical, mental, and emotional experience of it is quite another. I realised that until that moment I'd had no idea what my clients were talking about.

'Do you want a cup of tea?' one of them asked me.

My mouth was bone dry, my throat constricted. Tea would be nice. But I shook my head. No. How could I even contemplate doing something as normal as drinking tea, here in my living room, on my sofa, when these people had just told me that John was dead?

I rubbed my eyes. I couldn't focus. It was as if the world had slammed on its brakes and was starting to spin in reverse. Nothing made sense.

The officers continued with questions I had no clue how to answer.

'Did you notice anything odd in his behaviour?'

'Did he have mental health problems?'

I looked down at the floor and saw a dust bunny of dog hair. I felt suddenly embarrassed because I hadn't hoovered.

'Who can we call?' That question again.

The world now threatened to fall from its axis, roll away, and out of the universe forever. For what felt like an eternity, I couldn't think of anyone I wanted them to contact. In fact, part of me didn't want anyone else to join me in this nightmare. If anyone else knew, that would somehow make it real, and if it was real… well, I didn't want to inflict this pain on anyone else.

'Who shall we call? We won't leave you on your own. We'll stay until someone comes.'

So that was it. They needed to get away. Of course. They were at work. This was their job; telling an unsuspecting middle-aged woman her husband was dead and that the life we shared was over. Forever.

No, I suppose they couldn't leave me on my own.

I heard myself asking, 'What happened? Was it quick? Did he suffer?'

'The train was travelling at one hundred miles an hour.'

Train?

'He died instantly.'

When John left the house that morning, instead of going to see customers to do estimates, instead of deciding whether to do the jobs or come back home and rest as he'd said to me before he left, he drove three and half miles to Kelvedon railway station. He purchased an all-day parking ticket, made his way to the platform and climbed down onto the tracks, where he stood up and faced a one-hundred-mile-an-hour through train. Which, at 10:06 a.m., obliterated him.

The police officers told me they had a team that walked the half mile of train track between the point of impact and where the train finally came to a halt. They searched for what was left of John, photographing what they found, putting the remains into two body bags, then placing one bag inside the other.

'Who can we call?' That question. Again.

noone, I thought, and started rambling.

'You can't call Liam and Claudia. Liam's our son. They're going on a belated honeymoon at the weekend. Three weeks in Thailand. You can't call Phoebe. Our daughter. She won't cope.' And then, as if I'd forgotten what I'd just been told, 'It's mine and John's wedding anniversary on Saturday. We've been married for thirty-two years.'

But the police needed an answer. They needed to call someone to come and be with me so they could get on with things.

'Claudia,' I said finally. She would know what to do. 'But don't tell her what's happened.'

That's why Claudia got a call at work from the police, from my phone, with only the instruction to come to our home as soon as she could.

No, they couldn't give her any more details. But yes, it was urgent.

It would take Liam and Claudia at least an hour to get to me, especially if Claudia was at work and needed to pick Liam up from their flat at Borough Market. I tried to weigh up what would be worse: them doing that drive knowing that John was dead or having to fill in the mystery with their imaginations? Which was the lesser of these two evils?

'I have to call my son. I have to tell him myself.'

Liam answered almost immediately, totally oblivious to the fact that in the short space of time since our earlier phone conversation about contact lenses, which had been interrupted by a knock at the door, our lives as we knew them had ended.

'Who was at the door?' Liam asked, blissfully unaware. I tried to tell him but the words would not come. All I could say, punctuated by sobs, was, 'I'm sorry.'

One of the officers took the phone from me and, as kindly as possible, destroyed Liam's bliss.

In my living room the questions continued.

'Does anyone else live here with you?'

'Phoebe.'

'Where is she?'

'I don't know.'

I didn't know anything at that moment.

Phoebe had been going to visit a couple of friends that day but I had no idea where she might actually be at that precise moment. I did not want to call her. The thought of her attempting to drive after getting the news that her dad was dead terrified me. I must have voiced that thought out loud.

'If you find out where she is, we will go and get her.'

I wasn't actually in my body. I was watching and listening to the whole unreal scene as if it was happening to someone else.

Simultaneously, I was in more pain than I've ever experienced and also numb, unable to feel anything at all. I was floating through a foreign universe in an alternate reality.

Phoebe answered my call with her usual, 'Hey Mama.'

'Where are you?'

On hearing me, Phoebe's voice rose a full octave. 'Mum, what's wrong?'

'Where are you? Where are you?' I repeated, over and over, unable to say anything else for fear I would reveal the truth.

'Mum. Tell me what's wrong!' It broke my heart to hear the escalating panic in my daughter's voice, knowing what she was about to discover would break hers.

I opened my mouth to ask her, once again, where she was, but nothing at all came out. I held the phone towards the officer, who took it from me and walked from the room. I could hear the sound of his voice as he spoke to Phoebe but I couldn't make out the words.

This can't be real. This can't be happening. The words spun round on a loop in my head.

'There is a diary and pen on the front seat of your husband's car. He might have left a note. Is there a spare car key?'

Just twenty-four hours before, we'd spent a precious day with our grandchildren.

It was a standing joke between us that I was most definitely the second-best grandparent. The kids would have play arguments over who would sit next to whom at dinner. The loser got me. I really didn't mind. John was one of those people who was naturally great with children. He was effortlessly fun.

Neither the kids nor I had any idea when John had kissed them, hugged them, and waved them goodbye, that it would be the last time they would ever see him.

I had remained stuck to the same spot for I don't know how long, unable to move. I unglued my body from the sofa, went to the bin in the kitchen, and pulled out a crumpled piece of paper. It was a drawing John and Josh had done together the previous day. Just hours before the police had arrived, while tidying up, I had thrown it in the bin.

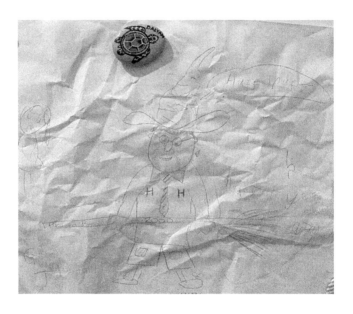

The simple drawing had suddenly taken on monumental significance. A piece of waste paper this morning forever transformed into a symbol of love, important beyond measure.

Smoothing out the crumples as best I could, I gazed at the picture before securing it with little magnets to the front of the fridge, a poignant reminder that none of us can ever be sure when we will do something for the very last time. John would never do another drawing with Josh. He would never play at being Hagrid, tricking Josh (aka Harry Potter) out of the precious golden snitch I'd bought from eBay. He'd never be Josh and Ruby's shop customer or Ruby's problem pupil again.

I returned to my spot on the sofa. Someone had moved John's slippers. I didn't know who or when. I simply noticed they were gone. Did they think it upset me to be sitting here staring at them? As if by moving them from my line of sight, it would somehow make this unbearable situation more… what? Bearable?

Everything was a blur. Like frames from a movie shuffled out of order, out of context. Making no sense. People came into and out of my field of vision like one of those time lapse special effects. I was in the centre, stock still while everything moved unnaturally fast around me, a lone figure framed by streaks and flashes of light and shadow.

I don't know in what order people arrived and I don't remember them leaving. The police left. The police came back. The events of that afternoon and evening happened in random flashes rather than in a linear progression of time. Through it all, I sat. Motionless. Rigid. A fixture on the sofa.

I looked into the faces of well-meaning people who arrived to give comfort, stricken expressions on their faces, but any comprehension I might have had for their despair couldn't get through my own wall of shock.

I heard Phoebe before I actually saw her. The sound she emitted was harrowing, like the howl of an injured animal, followed by a thud as she hit the floor.

Ally, Claudia's mum, arrived. Miranda, Claudia's sister, knelt on the floor in front of me, holding my hand, tears streaming down her face, shaking her head in disbelief.

Scot, Claudia's dad, was framed in the doorway while Ally made drinks for everyone. Scot's face was pale, his normally confident expression missing in action. *He's the same age as John,* I thought.

In the midst of emotional turmoil, men like them look for something to do. I imagined the tea towel held awkwardly in his hand was evidence of him drying up and searching unfamiliar cupboards to find where to put the cups away.

A doctor arrived. He perched on the edge of the other sofa and wrote out prescriptions. Diazepam for everyone. What made him think a prescription – a drug – would rectify this? Even in my shocked state, I knew that I was in the midst of the most devastating experience of my life, not sick, and not in need of further medication. After all I was still taking Prozac daily to keep my brain chemicals in balance.

'What good will Valium do?'

The doctor shrugged. What else was he supposed to do? I accepted the offered prescription but the last thing I wanted or needed was to be drugged. I envisioned taking a pill, going to sleep, and forgetting the brutal truth. How awful would it be to wake up and have to remember all over again that John was really dead? That this nightmare was indeed my real life now?

'Do you know if John was ill?' My question was met with a blank stare and then an expression of confusion. 'What I mean is, do you know if there was something wrong with John? Physically? Was he ill? Is that why he…'

'If you like, I'll check his medical records and either myself or one of the other doctors can give you a call.'

I heard the police explain about John's car, wallet, phone, and keys. Liam was calmly, rationally, grilling the police about how they knew for certain it was his dad. How did they know it wasn't a case of mistaken identity? How did they know his dad hadn't been mugged?

'That stuff could have been stolen,' Liam said. 'This doesn't make sense!'

The police explained that John had been formally identified by his fingerprints. I'd forgotten John had done some petty stuff way back in the past and his prints were on file.

So, we knew. It was definitely John.

Liam's voice broke and his tears began. 'Where is he? Where is my dad? I want to be with him.'

'He's in the mortuary at Colchester hospital but you can't see him.' The police officer shifted from one foot to the other. 'Well,' he continued, 'we can't actually stop you viewing the…' He cleared his throat. 'The body, if you insist. But we would strongly advise you not to.'

His words from earlier replayed in my mind. *The train was going at one hundred miles an hour.*

'I just want to be near my dad,' Liam said.

At some point, after it was dark and everyone else had gone, Phoebe and I were alone in the house. It felt almost possible, if I tried really hard, to pretend that nothing had happened. That John was just out somewhere and would be home shortly. That none of the other people had ever been there.

Phoebe and I were like walking, talking zombies. We took the dogs out for a walk. Our world had been devastated but the dogs still needed a walk before bed. I sorted the rubbish and put the bins out. Tuesday was bin day and John and I always put the bins out on Monday night. In the absence of knowing what else we should do, Phoebe and I did what was normal.

24

THE NEXT DAY

TUESDAY 30TH OCTOBER

FOR THE REST of the world, this was just another ordinary day. Other people were absorbed in mundane activities. Waking. Working. Shopping. Looking after children.

For me it was the beginning of a life I neither expected nor wanted. A life I had no idea how to live. It was the first day John was no longer in the world. He was dead. I was his widow. Everything had changed.

I had no idea what I was supposed to do or what came next.

My mind was at once paralysed and racing on overdrive. In the midst of this alien situation, I sought some understanding and perhaps some control. I tried to think. There had to be some explanation. There *had* to be something we didn't know about that tipped John over the edge.

Jim's stage-four cancer diagnosis was tragic but was it really what had driven John to kill himself? Surely not. John and I had been through so much in our lives together. We had faced and overcome so many challenges. Even during times of adversity, John and I always found a way through. We always survived. Together. As a team. Why was *now* different?

There was no precise timeline given for when I might get a call from the GP's surgery. So I could do nothing but wait to see if there was something going on with John's physical health that might shed some light. I was suspended in an unbearable limbo; my world had been upended. Everything had changed. Every nerve in my body felt shredded. My head pounded. My guts churned. My heart beat a rhythm of anxiety like nothing I'd ever experienced. Why was noone doing anything? It seemed like everyone else was going about their lives normally. As if nothing had happened.

What can I do?

There had to be something I could do to find answers, to locate the missing piece of the puzzle. Then, perhaps, I could make some sense of the nonsensical, terrifying situation I found myself in.

John was DEAD.

He had KILLED HIMSELF.

But WHY?

Frantically I rummaged through the cupboard where John kept his financial paperwork in untidy piles. I grabbed handfuls: bank statements; credit card statements; anything that looked like official letters or documents. I cleared the cupboard and dropped everything in a heap on the table.

After the frenzied activity, I paused and stood still and quiet. For a long time I just stared at the messy array of documents strewn across the table. Were the missing clues here? Perhaps John had money troubles that I didn't know about. Maybe it had become too much for him.

With a mixture of anticipation and dread, I sat down and started to read.

After some time, my heart sank and I slumped back in my seat. It was apparent these papers contained no revelations. No great unveiling of a secret that could shed light on why John had decided to end his own life so brutally.

Once again the sickening realisation that John was actually gone – forever – hit me like a physical punch to the gut. The tears started again. Not the pretty, silent, dignified tears you see delicate leading ladies weep in the movies but primal, harsh, guttural sobs.

Time passed, my sobbing subsided, and I sat staring into space.

'What about the sleeping tablets?' I asked noone in particular.

The doctor had prescribed John sleeping medication and antide-pressants.

I calculated that he must have been taking them for about nine days before he died. They hadn't seemed to help. In fact on reflection he'd seemed even more anxious. But I'd had blind faith they would somehow rebalance his sympathetic and parasympathetic nervous systems, reduce his anxiety, and allow him to sleep. That was what I believed: that the pills the doctor prescribed were medicines that would make John feel better.

I searched the kitchen until I found the sleeping pills where John had left them. They looked so insignificant. Tiny. Harmless. I picked up my phone and typed *Zopiclone and suicide* into the search bar.

Zopiclone tablets are sleeping pills (hypnotics) which work by acting on the brain to cause sleepiness[1]

Given my profession, a hypnotherapist, the irony of Zopiclone being a hypnotic was not lost on me. I continued to scan the results on the screen, seeing the first glimmer of an explanation that might make sense.

Side effects include: poor memory (amnesia). Seeing or hearing things that are not real (hallucinations). Thinking things that are not true (delusions). Feeling low or sad (depressed mood). Feeling physically or mentally tired. Agitation. Feeling confused. Feeling irritable or aggressive. Feeling restless or angry. Feeling light-headed or problems with coordination. Double vision. Moving unsteadily or staggering. Creeping on the skin (paraesthesia) Difficulty paying attention. Sleep-driving and other strange behaviour.[2]

I dropped my phone into my lap. I felt sick. Had John become suicidal as a result of the drugs he was given? John had been stressed and having trouble sleeping – a fairly normal reaction under the circumstances. But he was neither 'an insomniac' nor 'mentally ill'.

There have been some reports of people doing things while asleep that they do not remember when waking up after taking sleep medicine. This includes sleep driving and sleepwalking. Alcohol and some medicines for depression or anxiety can increase the chance that this serious effect will happen.[3]

Two things jumped out at me from the information I was scrolling through on my screen:

Sleep driving and other strange behaviour.

Some medicines for depression or anxiety can increase the chance that this serious effect will happen.

Next, I searched *hypnotics and suicide.*

The principal new contribution of this review is clarification regarding the timing of suicide risk related to ingestion of hypnotics. Under specific conditions hypnotics may induce or exacerbate suicidaility by altering consciousness or disinhibition at the time of peak drug effect.[4]

Continuing along the path of clues, it was like following a trail of breadcrumbs like in the fairy tale *Hansel and Gretel*, I returned to the kitchen cupboard and pulled out the other drug package – Citalopram. I returned to my chair and googled *Citalopram and suicide.*

Warning: Suicidal thoughts and behaviours. Citalopram use may increase suicidal thoughts or actions in some children, teenagers, or young adults within the first few months of treatment or when the dose is changed.[5]

I felt a sickening dread rising up through my body, enveloping my stomach, burning my throat, and flooding my already overflowing mind. If these drugs could make young people suicidal - maybe that is what they did to John? I continued reading.

Side Effects: Symptoms such as restlessness or difficulty in sitting or standing still can also occur during the first weeks of the treatment. Thoughts of suicide and worsening of your depression or anxiety disorder. If you are depressed and/or have anxiety disorders you can sometimes have thoughts of harming or killing yourself. These may be increased when first starting antidepressants.[6]

The description of the side effects, the time frame, all made sense. The balance of his mind had been altered by the very medication that was supposed to make him feel better. *Could that be it?* Had these drugs contributed to John's suicide?

I clicked the back button and began to explore the long list of search results. I read articles and studies from reputable sources like the *American Journal of Psychiatry*, *PubMed*, and others. The common threads were that the risk of suicide and violence is increased not only in young people but also when adults who had no mental health disorder take antidepressants and that the widespread belief that these drugs aren't dangerous for adults is a potentially lethal misconception. A wave of shock washed through me.

I devoured the information. I next found websites with accounts written by people whose loved ones had killed themselves after taking these drugs. Some of the survivors had set up pages or groups or organisations to help raise awareness about the dangers of the side effects. There's the Facebook page 'Stephen's Voice' set up to tell the story of Stephen O'Neill[7] who died following the onset of reactions that surfaced just twenty-four hours after he began taking the drugs: racing heart, strong agitation, a mind in overdrive with scary thoughts. There was AntiDepAware.co.uk, a site set up by a father to promote awareness of the dangers of anti-depressants following the death of his son.

"In 2009 my son, who had never been depressed in his life, went to see a doctor over insomnia caused by temporary work related stress. Contrary to NICE guidelines, he was prescribed Citalopram, and within days he died a violent death."[8]

Why had the doctor prescribed antidepressants as well as sleeping pills to John? It seemed an odd combination: Citalopram, an SSRI (or selective serotonin re-uptake inhibitor) antidepressant with a side effect of insomnia, and Zopiclone, a sleeping pill with a side effect of causing depression?

Another anomaly I discovered is that SSRIs are prescribed for both depression and anxiety. But these are such different psychological conditions. Almost opposite ends of the emotional spectrum. I shared my discoveries with Phoebe, Claudia, and Liam.

'It's like a car tyre,' said Liam, shaking his head as if to try and comprehend. 'Depression is like a flat that needs more air. Anxiety is a tyre that's already over-inflated. If you give it more air it will eventually explode.'

---

1. 'Patient Information for Zopiclone.' Package Leaflet. Accessed July 2021. https://bit.ly/3hPMyg9
2. Ibid.
3. Ibid.
4. McCall, W Vaughn et al., 'Hypnotic Medications and Suicide: Risk, Mechanisms, Mitigation, and the FDA'. *The American Journal of Psychiatry* vol. 174,1 (2017): 18-25. doi:10.1176/appi.ajp.2016.16030336
5. 'Patient Information for Citalopram.' Package Leaflet. Accessed July 2021. https://bit.ly/3dXNVIj

6. Ibid.
7. Stephen's Voice. Community Facebook Page. https://www.facebook.com/stephenoneillsvoice
8. AntiDepAware: Promoting awareness of the dangers of antidepressants. Accessed July 2021. https://bit.ly/3r10los

25

THE BIRDS STILL SANG

IN THE MORNINGS, John would almost always be the first to wake up. With eyes tight shut, I'd pretend to be asleep, happy to remain in the warm comfort of our bed, listening to the sound of the bird-song outside for just a bit longer. He knew how to cajole me into getting up, reminding me in a unique way that our dogs needed a walk.

'Come on, you lazy bitch,' he'd announce, pulling the covers off me. 'There's arses to be wiped!' An intentionally inappropriate paraphrasing of a reference to a comedy show we enjoyed. Like so many of our inside jokes, it would make absolutely no sense to anyone except us two.

We could engage in entire conversations with only a few intelligible words, loads of stupid jokes, and the look in our eyes. We had unconsciously developed our own kind of private, short-hand language.

Now, I was alone in our bed. The birds still sang outside the bedroom window but I no longer heard them. I did not wake up in a warm snoozy daze that I'd happily extend for as long as possible. Instead, I was violently launched into consciousness, heart pounding, mind racing. Evidence that even in the depths of sleep there was a part of my brain that was struggling to make some sense of things. The gut-wrenching, painful anxiety yanked me into wakefulness. It was like someone had attached jump leads to my heart.

When the police had returned John's car, they parked it on the drive. In the same spot where John would have. Not in exactly the right position, but close enough that when I saw it, part of my mind fell for the cruel trick that John had returned home. Handing me the keys, the police had solemnly confirmed they'd searched through the diary they found on the front seat – alongside a pen – but that there was no communication from John. No goodbye. No suicide note. No explanation.

Not yet fully awake, my mind threw up an idea. If John had actually *planned* to kill himself, somewhere in this very house, he might have left me a note.

Throwing back the covers, I raced into my office. I knew exactly what I was looking for; the fire proof container where we stored important paperwork and documents like our marriage certificate, passports, and birth certificates. Flinging open the cupboard, I started pulling out books, binders, papers, folders, boxes, and bits and bobs in search of it. *This is where he would have left a note.* I was sure of it. I felt a jolt of both anticipation and fear at the thought of reading what John might have written in his farewell letter to me.

I searched the container frantically then tipped the contents out on the floor.

There was no note.

'What are you doing?' Phoebe stood framed in the doorway, confusion and concern on her face.

'Looking for a suicide note,' I sobbed.

'You won't find a note, Mum,' Phoebe said, gently placing her hand on my shoulder. 'Because Dad wasn't planning on killing himself. He didn't want to die. He just wanted to feel better.'

I'd never understood why people brought food to the bereaved. Now, I know. In those early days, if people hadn't been kind enough to turn up at the door with prepared meals and bags of shopping, we simply wouldn't have eaten.

Noone seemed to know what to say, except how shocked they were.

'John? Really?'

'John? I can't believe it!'

noone knew what to do, except to try and sustain us with gifts of food.

Sitting at the kitchen table one evening, surrounded by an assortment of casserole dishes that didn't belong in my kitchen, I smiled. 'John would have loved all this great food.'

Being one of a family of seven children, with parents for whom money was often tight, he never shook off the habit of eating everything on his plate really fast. Just so noone else would take it, and so he was ready in case any seconds were on offer.

I was still waiting for the GP to call regarding John's medical records. I needed to know: was his illness in Santorini actually something sinister? Had he been hiding the truth from me? And I had new questions, too, about his prescriptions.

The two days that had passed since John's death felt at once like an eternity and as though no time had passed at all. We were in limbo. Waiting but with no real idea of what for. Some kind of sign? For John to come home and for this to have been a nightmare?

It was already dark outside, the garden beyond barely visible through the windows. Inside, the lighting was soft and warm. Liam and Claudia had returned to their home. Phoebe and I were sitting opposite each other at the table when my phone rang. The number flashed up on the screen confirming it was the doctor's surgery. This was the call I had been waiting for.

Clouded with confusion, emotion, and my newly-acquired information about the side effects of combining antidepressants and sleeping tablets, I did not trust myself to be able to accurately relay the conversation. For that reason, I clicked to enable the loudspeaker so that Phoebe could join in on the call – or at least listen to what was said.

It soon became apparent that the doctor and I were talking at cross-purposes. I was attempting to establish whether John had been ill. The doctor was talking about John's last consultation and emphasising that he'd done nothing wrong by not seeing John in person.

I tried to bring the conversation back to the subject of whether, on our return from Athens, John had been given some horrible diagnosis, perhaps terminal. Even though, in my mind, that scenario didn't really add up, I had to explore the possibility.

'Did anything show up on the X-ray or ECG?'

'No,' the doctor said, switching once again to John's most recent consultation, just before he died. Again, he mentioned having adhered to the UK's National Institute for Health and Care Excellence (NICE) guidelines.

Phoebe locked eyes with me. I could see from her expression that we had both come to the same understanding.

'Are you telling me you didn't actually see John… in the same room… face-to-face?' I wanted to be quite sure I hadn't misunderstood.

The doctor sounded uncomfortable. Defensive even. 'That's right. We had a telephone consultation. It's common practice.'

Common practice, maybe, but was it the most appropriate course of action?

The doctor admitted he didn't know John and wasn't sure they had ever met. (It later transpired he had in fact seen John once during the five years he was registered with this doctor's surgery.) He continued to waffle on about having had special training in mental health and conducting phone consultations.

Did that training give you superpowers to see through the fucking phone line? I thought.

All I had wanted to know, when I'd arranged for this call, was if John was unwell and hadn't told me. Since then, I'd acquired new information about the medication this doctor had prescribed. And now, his caginess about never having seen John face-to-face prompted new questions. Ones that were swirling and spinning in my mind, not yet cogent enough for me to ask out loud.

If John was sick enough to be given powerful psychiatric drugs, how come he wasn't sick enough to warrant a face-to-face appointment?

How can you examine a patient if you do not see them?

If you do not examine them, how can you diagnose them?

If you cannot effectively diagnose them then how, with all good conscience, can you prescribe a course of pharmaceutical treatment?

I pulled my thoughts back to my original purpose of the call.

'So just to be absolutely clear. There was nothing wrong with John, physically?'

'Not as far as the test results show.'

'You gave him sleeping tablets and antidepressants?'

'Yes.'

'If John wasn't sleeping because he was depressed, the antidepressants would have sorted that, wouldn't they?'

'Possibly.'

'And if John had insomnia, which was leading him to feel depressed from lack of sleep, then the sleeping pills would be the obvious answer?'

Into the silence, I continued. 'I just don't understand why you gave him both?' The rising inflection of my voice turned my statement into a question.

I decided to ask his opinion, as a medic, on the discoveries I had made about the link between suicide and antidepressant drugs, especially SSRIs.

'What you're suggesting is certainly within the realm of possibility,' he conceded. 'In rare cases, a small number of people who take Citalopram experience side effects including suicidal or self-harming thoughts, especially during the first fourteen days.'

Once again, I met Phoebe's gaze.

'But, if anything,' the doctor continued, 'I would say it was the sleeping pills that were more likely to cause problems. They can put people into a kind of zombified state.'

'If John had been reassured that it's perfectly normal to have trouble sleeping in response to bad news, do you think that might have helped normalise and humanise his experience?' I couldn't help but think that if the doctor had done this, rather than prescribe mind-altering drugs, John might still be alive.

I heard the doctor sigh, as if growing weary of the conversation. 'The fact is, Mrs Collins, depressed people kill themselves.'

I was stunned, as if his words had physically struck me. That was the point: John had been *distressed*, but not *depressed*.

Signalling that the time he'd allotted for the call was up, the doctor changed the subject, expressing concern now for my mental state.

'Shall we schedule another call, just so I can check in on how you're doing?'

In a bit of a haze, I agreed and wrote down the date and time to ensure I didn't forget. The doctor affirmed he'd call me on the appointed day and we hung up.

Phoebe and I sat in silence. Looking out of the window into the darkness enveloping the garden, no matter how hard I tried to shed some light on what had happened, I remained in the dark.

26

THE RED BLANKET

I FELT like a single grain of sand on a beach facing an oncoming tsunami.

In my new reality, the days and nights all blended into one. I was lost, alone, and utterly terrified.

One night, Phoebe was in my bed with me, on John's side, while Liam and Claudia slept in Phoebe's room. Phoebe became hysterical. Her crying turned to sobs and the sobs turned to a stream of words about what it meant that her dad was gone – forever. Claudia and Liam appeared, trying to comfort her.

I shouted, 'Stop it. I can't take this! I can't have you do this. Stop it. Just stop it.'

None of us really slept. Existence had become a living, waking nightmare. I dreaded going to sleep; scared of dreaming that reality was only a dream and then waking up to find, once again, that I had been cruelly tricked.

Not being able to see John's body made it harder to accept he was actually dead. It deepened my disbelief and emotional distress, if that was possible. Then it dawned on me; John's identity had been confirmed by fingerprints. *That means a hand must still be intact.* Gruesome as it was, Liam, Claudia, Phoebe and I needed to see *something* of John, even a body part, in order to help us process the fact he was never coming back. If a hand was all we could see, so be it.

Arrangements were made and we travelled to the hospital to visit the morgue. Walking from the car toward the hospital entrance, I watched people fussing about at the machines trying to purchase tickets for the car park, others entering and leaving the hospital, and I wondered about all the reasons that might have brought them there.

Maybe they were visiting newborn babies and their proud new mums. Maybe they were attending the hospital for treatment. Perhaps they were visiting the sick or were there to collect someone well enough to go home. So many reasons to be in this place at this time.

We made our way along brightly lit corridors following signs for the morgue. Once there, we introduced ourselves to the young woman whose job it was to guide us through the process. She made us tea, kindly explaining the process and then patiently listening while we spoke about John. When Liam showed her photos of his dad, her eyes misted.

Opening the door to the room where John's remains were, she reminded us not to try to hold his hand. *Because it's no longer attached to anything,* I thought.

A red blanket hung over a dark blue body bag on a silver trolley. Resting on the blanket was John's hand, placed to look as if his body was beneath the blanket and his hand merely resting on top. But it wasn't quite in the right place.

John's hands, especially his fingernails, were distinctive, unmistakable. I'd know them anywhere. It was undoubtedly him.

Remember when you held the kids' hands? When you held hands with the grandchildren? With me? Remember holding the handlebar of your Harley? The steering wheel of your car? A tool when you were working? A cup of coffee? A glass of wine? Cutlery as you ate your 'favourite all-time dinner'?

Through silent tears we took it in turns to use our phones to take photos of our hands gently touching John's bruised and battered fingers, a sad record of our final physical contact with John in this life. What remained of John, at least what had been recovered from the tracks, was in that room, in that body bag, under that blanket with us.

There was a horrible smell engulfing the room, rank and pungent. It was the fragrance of death. Was it real? Or was it some olfactory hallucination created by my imagination at the knowledge of what, or how little, actually remained of John's body?

We each said our goodbyes. Liam was at pains to make sure we each stayed for as long as we needed to, to connect with John's essence, his spirit. It was as if we had come to get him, to take him back with us.

John was gone. The reality that I'd never see him again hit me like a tidal wave, tossing me head over heels, filling my lungs with the murky waters of loss and grief. His life was finished and so was mine. I was still breathing. My heart still beating. My body was alive, but life as I knew it had ended at the same moment that train hit John.

27

A HUMMINGBIRD AND A HARLEY

'WHO IS YOUR FUNERAL DIRECTOR?' I remember an anonymous person from the coroner's office asking me on one of the dozens of phone calls I would have with them.

Who is your funeral director? Like I have a favourite on speed dial.

My life was in turmoil but the grim reality was there were *arrangements* that needed to be made. Attending to the practicalities of my deceased husband's affairs messed with my mind. My memory couldn't hold on to all the details. The cognitive capacity I needed to do things like complete John's final self-employed tax return, cancel his memberships to various trade organisations, and deal with his bank and credit cards, all while feeling like life itself was utterly pointless, was a confusing juxtaposition to say the least.

In those darkest early days, every time the post dropped through the letterbox, it brought more official letters. An avalanche of officialdom and legalities, tasks to be completed and questions to be answered – at the point in my life where I was least capable. I was exhausted and barely able to keep my head above water. Even the simplest task seemed like an application to Mensa.

I called the only funeral director I knew; the one local to our old home, who had dealt with Dad's funeral.

Through tears, stumbling over my words, I tried my best to explain what had happened and why I was calling. I wanted to hear, *Oh yes, of course we remember you and your dad.* I was hoping for some words of recognition, which I thought would make the whole horrible experience a little more bearable. A bit more human.

Instead, they put me on hold.

I hung up.

I was territorial in my grief. I didn't want anyone intruding on it. It was hell but it was *my* hell. John had been wrenched from my life and, in a perverse way, I felt I needed to protect my grieving process in a way I hadn't been able to protect John. An introvert at heart, the last thing I wanted was a public event attended by people who thought they *ought* to be there, whether out of respect or worrying about being *seen* to pay respects. This was our family's tragedy and I didn't want anyone holidaying on our misery. No, there would be no comfort had from people paying their respects.

I googled 'direct cremation'. No service. No ceremony. Nothing. Just collect the ashes when it's done. If it was good enough for David Bowie, it'd be good enough for John. I discussed it with Phoebe and Liam, but they weren't sure. So, we explored the idea of something private – just for us – but with something more. I continued my internet search.

I lost count of the number of photos I saw of sombre black limousines and logos that incorporated doves or angel's wings. Then I came across a Smart car. I stopped scrolling and clicked the link for Freedom Funerals. Yes, it was a Smart car with Freedom Funerals and a dolphin emblazoned on the side.

Just a year earlier, I had decided I wanted a Smart car. John did all the research about the pros and cons of different models and together we travelled around taking test drives. On the day we bought 'Arthur Car' (AKA 'half a car') the Smart car, we had lunch in an Italian café while waiting for it to be valeted. I admired some jewellery in the window of a little independent shop. For no reason other than because we wanted to, John treated me to an intricate silver and amethyst bangle and a silver necklace with a lapis lazuli hummingbird pendant.

Freedom Funerals use of the Smart car seemed to be a sign. Clicking through to the website, I noted it wasn't situated on a high street with headstones and angels in a dusty window display, but on an industrial estate. John would have loved the simplicity and practicality of that. Another sign?

Sitting on the same sofa I'd been on when that knock on the door came, I made the call. As soon as Paul answered, the difference was instantly apparent. I talked and he listened. Then he talked and I listened. He told me the story of why he'd started Freedom Funerals.

'When my mum died,' he explained, 'we got the funeral we were sold rather than the funeral we wanted.'

'And why a dolphin?'

'Most funeral directors use doves as a symbol, but doves are dopey creatures. Dolphins are clever and beautiful.'

I found myself smiling. Paul answered all my questions and listened to me with kindness and compassion. 'Come and see the chapel where we would look after John,' he invited. 'Then you'll know if we're right for you.'

At last; this was something I could do during the unreal, nightmarish, otherwise-in-limbo time I found myself in.

So, Phoebe, Liam, Claudia, and I set off to visit Freedom Funerals, to see the Chapel of Rest on an industrial estate, with the promotional Smart cars parked outside.

As soon as we stepped inside I knew we were in the right place. It was beautiful in a very unconventional way. It provided a brief and welcome respite from the agony we were living through. There was an impressive array of symbols and iconography on offer. A Christian cross, an Egyptian cat deity, a pentagram, and Sponge Bob Square Pants!

'I like to cover all bases,' Paul smiled, 'or none.'

The Chapel of Rest was a simple white room with chairs and a trolley for the coffin to rest on. There was a sense of peace which triggered new tears of relief. In the midst of all the madness we were living, something felt strangely right.

We talked about John. Not just what had happened, not just the grim details of his death, but his life. Funny stories, what he was like. The fact that while he'd been raised Catholic, he didn't practice any religion.

It struck me like a thunderbolt that there would never be any new stories or anecdotes. We could never make any new memories. All we had now were re-runs of old ones.

'What's with the Harley?' Liam asked, jerking me out of the mental labyrinth I was lost in.

I couldn't believe it when Paul showed us the gleaming chrome Harley Davidson motorcycle with the specially constructed side car adapted to carry a coffin. I smiled, thinking of how John customised his Harley, transforming it from its original teal and cream to a glittering red, replacing the pipes and handle bars. I thought about him roaring off down Crescent Road to a rally or a ride out. I remembered how delighted he'd been when, in 2008, his bike won 'Best Sportster' at the HOG (Harley Owner's Group) Essex Chapter bike show. As he proudly showed me the big shiny gold trophy, he said, 'I don't think I've ever won anything before.' I could hardly believe this memory, fresh as the morning's rain, was ten years ago.

While we admired the bike and said how much John would love it, Phoebe nudged me. 'Mum! Look.'

I glanced in the direction she was pointing. On the side of the large industrial container was a metal decoration, the type you generally find hanging in the garden. I took a closer look.

It was a purple hummingbird. Purple is my favourite colour. And the hummingbird had been a part of my company name since 2007. Right next to the hummingbird was a magnetic Las Vegas gambling chip, also purple. We all loved Vegas, especially Phoebe, who had been there several times. John and I had spent the 'best week of his life' there and it was where Jim accompanied us for Liam's twenty-first birthday when John and I renewed our wedding vows.

Even to me, someone who professed to have no particular spiritual beliefs, these signs provided a certain comfort. Until that moment, I hadn't realised just how badly I needed that.

'For someone who you say didn't believe in an afterlife, John seems to be sending you some pretty heavy hints!' Paul said with a soft smile.

Certain that we were in the right place, we discussed potential dates and arrangements.

'What's your most basic coffin?' My question didn't come from a place of miserly meanness. I just knew John's views on wasting outlandish amounts of money on such things.

'MDF. And to be perfectly honest with you, all coffins are just MDF under whatever fancy veneer people choose.'

Paul showed us the MDF coffin. Liam took a deep breath in. 'It reminds me of a thousand trips to DIY stores with Dad,' he said.

John was a practical man. The kind of man who could make things and mend things. He often said if I came up with an idea, he could find a way to make it. Of all the things he'd crafted and made over the years, many were made from MDF. It made me smile. Another sign for a non-believer?

We chose a beautiful hand-crafted slate urn on which we could write messages in chalk. 'I'm going to keep his ashes in the living room on the shelf above the log burner,' I announced. I hadn't thought about this until that precise moment, but suddenly knew it was right.

My dad's funeral several years before had been a true celebration of his life. John, together with our sons and my nephew, carried his coffin. There was music by Dolly Parton and Monty Python. I sat between Mum and Auntie Olive, holding their hands. John delivered a touching eulogy about how my dad was not just his father-in-law but his friend.

In 2016, at Olive's funeral, there was 'Nessun Dorma' and 'Don't Worry Be Happy' and stories of respect, admiration, and love.

John's funeral was like neither of these. In fact, it was like none I'd ever attended before. Yet it was perfect in its uniqueness.

We returned to Freedom Funerals the evening prior to the cremation. Paul let us into the chapel and told us to stay as long as we wanted to. We placed photos of John on top of his coffin, including one of him smiling broadly while sat astride his Harley at the bike show where he'd won the trophy. By then it had been customised and the teal and cream paintwork replaced by sparkling red. John wore dark shades, a bandana, and a leather waistcoat.

We lit incense in his favourite fragrance: nag champa.

Sitting on the floor, we pulled out pens and markers and set about decorating the coffin with doodles and personally meaningful quotes. We wrote messages and drew symbols while sharing memories and heart-warming stories. We let our tears flow as freely as our creativity.

Inside the now-customised coffin, we placed letters Ruby and Josh had written to their grandpa. When the time felt right, we said goodnight and went home to try to sleep.

Early the next morning, as we returned to Freedom Funerals to add a few more messages to the coffin. the sky was – to borrow a phrase from John – the most magnificent 'sky-blue-pink'.

After writing our final messages, we all helped move the coffin from the Chapel of Rest to the side car of the Harley.

Claudia once again taking the driving seat, we followed the Harley – ridden by Paul and carrying John on his final ride out to the crematorium gardens – watching the sunlight reflected in the shiny polished chrome. We stood together in the gardens and hugged each other while John's body was being cremated. More tears flowed. Few words were exchanged. We stayed until the time felt right to leave.

At home we drank tea and ate doughnuts. We went for a simple lunch and whiled away the time until we got a call from the crematorium to tell us that it was time; we could collect John's ashes and bring him home.

28

THE PLACE WHERE HE DIED

I STARED BLANKLY out of the window during the ten-minute drive from our home to Kelvedon station. We drove past familiar places: the garden centre; houses; the pub; the place where we bought our dog food. *What had he been thinking?*

I tried to imagine what could have been going through John's mind when he made this same journey just twenty-five days before.

He'd driven his car on these very roads. These roads had taken him to the station. Taken him to his death. On a journey from which he would never return. A journey that would forever change the course of my life. Of all our lives.

Claudia parked the car and we got out. The clouds that had allowed the sun to peek through earlier that morning were merging together.

'Where did the police say Dad parked?' I asked, unsure they'd actually said.

'Up there, at the end.' Liam pointed then tucked his hand back into his pocket.

'Why would he park there?'

'I guess the car park would have been full of commuters on a Monday morning?' A statement and a question all rolled into one.

We walked to where John had left his car for the very last time, and entered the platform.

Kelvedon station is small and anonymous. Unremarkable and uninteresting. Just two platforms: one for trains bound for London, the other for those wishing to travel in the opposite direction out of Essex towards Suffolk. I glanced around at the ordinary scene and tried once more to imagine what might have been going through John's mind.

The grey of the concrete platform mirrored the oppressive grey of the November sky. I glanced down at the cold train tracks, silver with black oily streaks. The surrounding gravel was dirty, covered in a powdery black residue, stray pieces of nondescript litter blowing about.

Twenty-five days before, this was where John's life ended. Of all the places in the world he had been, this was where he died. I tried not to imagine his final moments. I tried not to picture those two officers walking along the tracks retrieving body parts and placing them into body bags. But I couldn't help myself from wondering: *How could they possibly be sure they had found and retrieved every part of John's body?*

I recalled one of the morbid searches I'd typed into google: *What happens to someone hit by a train?*

Google's answer: *Pretty much the same as when a bug hits your windscreen when you're driving on a motorway.*

I looked at Phoebe, Liam, and Claudia, wondering why we were putting ourselves through this. Did we hope that by retracing John's final steps we might gain new insight into his state of mind on that fateful day?

Liam appeared solemn, lost in thought. Claudia watched him closely, as if she wanted to ensure he didn't connect too deeply with his father's experience. A train thundered past. Phoebe winced, pulling her coat tighter around herself, closing her eyes, shutting out the world which had turned so hostile.

The officer accompanying us read from papers flapping on a clip-board. Her description of John's last known movements were punctuated by uncertain sounding *umm*'s and *arr*'s as she looked from the clipboard, to the track, to us, and back to the clipboard.

'Just be honest with us,' Liam implored. 'Nothing you say can hurt us any more than we are already.'

Once again, she glanced down at her notes. I wondered if she was being hesitant to spare our feelings or if she just didn't know what she was doing. She muttered something about viewing the CCTV.

The four of us, together with the officer, walked the length of the platform and up and over the footbridge to the small ticket office situated on the London-bound platform. The woman working there set about trying to locate the recordings of the CCTV from October

29th. She was helpful and sympathetic, but it soon became clear it was impossible for her to assist us while still dealing with requests for tickets and information from members of the public. A near constant stream of curious commuters gazed quizzically at us through the glass partition. I imagined each of them speculating about the reasons we might be there.

Suddenly the walls of the ticket office closed in. The desire to escape overwhelmed me. I wanted to go home. Right away. Phoebe was white as a sheet. Liam remained focussed on the task in hand.

Eventually, the officer said she would try to arrange a visit to the transport police station in Colchester for another day so we could view the CCTV footage.

'We want Dad's stuff,' Liam said as we walked back outside. 'You said you have his phone, his wallet, and his wedding ring.'

'I'm not sure we can give them to you.' The officer looked uncomfortable. 'They're considered... a bio-hazard.'

The implication of her words sickened me and I felt the breath catch in my throat.

'We want his property,' Liam said, his tone uncompromising.

On the way back to the car, once again, we retraced John's final steps. I glanced at the last bench on the platform. Looking at the innocuous object, which for me now had such significance, I tried to imagine what could possibly have been going on in John's mind when he sat there.

29

JOHN'S FINAL MOMENTS

WHILE THE REST of the world prepared gifts and lights and decorations for Christmas, Claudia drove us to the transport police station in Colchester to view the CCTV footage from the day John died. She'd stepped in to do all the driving because Liam, Phoebe, and I were all reluctant to get behind the wheel. I was constantly distracted, my confidence at rock bottom as a driver and in most other areas of my life too.

The transport police station was a nondescript building, which we had trouble finding. Once inside we were shown into a gloomy anonymous room. There was a table, upon which sat a small portable TV and video player.

'Some of the cameras at the station are not... operational,' said the police officer who had met us at Kelvedon station as she fiddled with the video player and TV. 'So we can't see things from more than one angle I'm afraid. The quality of the film isn't that great, either.'

'But you can see it's definitely my dad?' Liam asked. He was keen to know everything; to be as fully informed as possible. It was his way of trying to regain some control and make some sense of what had happened.

She nodded. 'I'll stop the footage just before…' She searched for the right word. 'Just before… impact.'

Without removing our coats, we huddled around the small TV screen.

I felt sick. I took a sideways glance at Phoebe. She looked terrified. None of us knew what to expect.

The footage was grainy and jerky in places, as if a series of still photos had been strung together. But what we were witnessing was undeniable: the final moments of John's life.

We watched John enter Platform Two from the car park and walk in the direction of the footbridge that leads to Platform One and the London-bound trains. This was a journey John had made several times as he travelled to visit Jim in the preceding weeks.

Silently we fixed our collective gaze on the screen. We watched John pause before reaching the footbridge then turn around and head back in the direction he'd just come, like perhaps he'd changed his mind about something.

At that moment, a non-stop freight train hurtled through the station. I could vividly recall the feeling of being on a platform when such a train thunders past: that sudden rush of air, the rever-berating sound, the vacuum sensation. I watched as John stepped back further into the yellow safety area of the platform.

'If he'd intended to kill himself, would that not have been the perfect opportunity?' Liam pointed to the screen but looked directly at the police officer, who didn't reply.

Then John walked down the platform, back toward the entrance to the car park.

At the last bench on the platform, he sat down. He remained there for a few minutes, apparently looking down at his phone, before getting to his feet and continuing toward the car park. Through the grainy CCTV we watched John stop and turn forty-five degrees to face the track head-on. The train that would kill him was visible in the distance.

The footage jerked from a frame showing John standing on the platform to one with him standing on the track a few seconds before the train hits.

'It doesn't show how my dad actually ended up on the track. Play it again,' Liam insisted. The officer paused, rewound, and replayed the section several times. The footage did not show how John got from the platform onto the track.

Did he jump? Did he step off the platform? Did he climb down? Did he trip and fall? We didn't get any answers from the CCTV footage.

As we left the building and made our way back towards the car, I felt a kind of relief, not merely because the ordeal was over but also because, after seeing John in the footage, his final moments played out in that grainy black and white CCTV, I was even more certain he had not gone to the station that day intending to end his life.

30

HAPPY IS THE WRONG WORD

THE CALL from the doctor to check on how I was doing never came. He'd forgotten. I emailed the doctor's surgery and for the third time requested John's medical records, pointing out the doctor had failed to call me as agreed.

He called later that evening and apologised. I reiterated my concerns about the drugs. Since our first discussion I'd discovered even more evidence supporting the idea of suicide resulting from the negative side effects of prescription drugs, especially SSRI antidepressants. Again I asked him, as a professional, as a medic, and as the person who knew enough about the drugs to prescribe them, whether he was familiar with the information I was only just discovering about these drugs.

His response was curt:

'Should I be contacting my legal representative?'

'I don't know, should you?' I wasn't accusing him of any wrong doing and I wasn't planning to sue him.

'You seem to think the drugs I prescribed are the reason your husband is dead.'

'I believe they were a significant contributing factor,' I said. 'Don't you?'

He sidestepped the question and offered to call me again.

'Or we could meet, if you'd prefer?'

We set a date and time for the in-person meeting. *Ironic,* I thought, disconnecting the call, *that he's asking me to meet him face-to-face, when he never asked John.*

Liam and I sat side by side in the waiting room of the doctor's surgery, the long black winter coat John had bought me years before helping to ward away the chill in both the air and the atmosphere. Liam was well dressed, handsome and smart as usual. I looked around at the other people in the waiting room, beginning to feel envious of their mundane reasons for seeing their GP. I caught myself. What did I know? I had no idea what anyone else was going through; we all have our own battles to fight. None of us truly knows what another is going through.

The doctor called us in. We were desperate for information. For answers. For a way to make sense of what had happened. I didn't trust my ability to recall the details of the discussion, and Phoebe and Claudia would be keen to know what the doctor had to say. So, before taking a seat, I pressed record on the audio setting on my phone and placed it on the desk between us.

I asked the doctor how John had seemed during the telephone consult nine days before he died.

'Relaxed,' the doctor replied, folding his arm. 'Not objectively depressed or anxious. Normal, natural, but down. He sounded…' he paused before continuing. 'Happy is perhaps the wrong word. But I'd say he was stable.' He confirmed, in his professional opinion, he hadn't considered John to be in any danger of harming himself.

If John was psychologically *stable* enough not be considered a suicide risk, and if he was psychologically *stable* enough not to need a face-to-face consultation, why was he *unstable* enough to need a prescription for mind altering drugs; antidepressants and sleeping pills?

Instead of referring John for counselling support, instead of asking about and advising John on sleep hygiene, the doctor had gone straight to prescribing sleeping tablets at the highest dosage, together with the SSRI antidepressant. When I queried this, he assured me it was common practice. Standard even.

'I've read about cases where drugs taken together combine to create an iatrogenic reaction,' Liam said, revealing more about the extent of our research, from which we'd discovered that an illness or reaction caused by a medication or a physician is said to be 'iatrogenic'.[1]

'I can't honestly exclude that as a possibility,' the doctor admitted. 'I absolutely can't.'

As the meeting came to a conclusion, I picked up my phone and stopped recording.

The doctor offered his condolences, saying how distraught he felt. He described how he'd talked about John's case with his wife, also a GP. He said she had categorically reassured him he'd done nothing wrong.

Nice for you, I thought, *to have your spouse to talk things over with, to get the kind of reassurance only they can offer.*

'One more question.' I sensed him tense. 'If you could go back and do that call with John over, would you do anything differently?'

He paused for no more than a few seconds then shook his head. 'No.'

In light of everything, I found that response arrogant, alarming, and tragic. To me, it suggested the doctor believed there was nothing to learn from John's death, and therefore no opportunity to prevent it from happening to someone else.

---

1. Shiel, William C. Jr., MD, FACP, FACR. "Medical Definition of Iatrogenic." Medicine.Net. Accessed July 2021. https://bit.ly/3yDkMu0

31

TWO DUVETS

ALONE AND NO LONGER BELONGING TO a side, I now occupied the space in the centre of our king size bed. I had taken to piling a second duvet on top of the usual one. The additional weight pressing down on my body provided some inexplicable comfort.

Enveloped in a tangle of quilts, wrapped around me like a nest, I was a creature preparing for hibernation. Wishing I could sleep until this unbearable season was over.

Two duvets was a strange and simple way to counter the lonely isolation of a bed intended for two that now held only me. My mind drifted to thoughts and memories, seemingly unrelated, yet always following a similar thread, even if consciously I was unaware of quite what that was.

A memory I had not thought about in decades popped to the front of my mind. I was little, probably around five years old. I remember holding my mum's hand and looking up at her as she spoke to another lady who had 'lost her husband'.

In hushed tones my mum asked her, 'How are you?'

'I put his pyjama top on a pillow,' the woman confided. 'I sleep with it on his side of the bed. It makes me think he's still here with me.' She started to cry, silent tears she dabbed at with a cotton handkerchief. 'Silly, isn't it?'

I squeezed my mum's hand a little tighter. Even then, as a little girl with limited comprehension of the secret ways of the adult world, that description of the pillow and the PJs made me so sad.

Our once beloved home descended into a world of untidy, dusty chaos. Any purpose for undertaking routine chores, the simple things that keep a home going, totally gone. Piles of laundry covered the floor of our bedroom, including the clothes John had taken off the night before he died. Things that were previously so very important now seemed utterly trivial.

I'd developed an aversion to venturing out, even a trip to the local supermarket, so the fridge was a sorrowfully vacant space, with no sign now of people bringing food. It was reminiscent of those long ago days I'd experienced as a single parent when John had remarked, 'You've never got any food.'

The bed remained unmade, the sheets in desperate need of changing. Some days I didn't bother to shower, brush my hair or even my teeth. Unable to sleep, I'd lie in bed googling things like: *side effects of SSRIs.* I found myself unable to refrain from conducting more morbid searches, such as the accounts of drivers of trains that had hit people.

Every so often I was struck by what I can only describe as raw panic and pain. The realisation that this tragic, sudden, unendurable loss was indeed real.

Like being hit by a train, I thought.

People use that phrase when trying to describe overwhelming shock. Now I understood all too well the use of that particular metaphor.

Never before had I felt so totally alone. Our home, which I'd often said was too small, now felt unbearably enormous and so empty. Lifeless.

It was warm for November, the bright afternoon sun hung low in the sky. I'd forced myself to venture out. I sat alone in a coffee shop, a medium wet latte in a takeaway cup on the table in front of me. I'd done this – sat by myself in a coffee shop – loads of times before. But this was my first time as a widow.

'Wonderful Christmas Time' played over the shop speakers, although noone was really listening. I watched an unsmiling barista create festive concoctions piled high with squirty cream and flashes of gold spray.

Outside in the car park, at the top of a leafless tree, perched a solitary crow squawking loudly. A memory drifted through my mind from the previous Christmas Eve. 'What do you get the woman who has everything?' John had smiled.

I'd been intrigued by examples of stuffed birds and animals on loan to my tattooist, the work of an eccentric local taxidermist, so I'd suggested a visit to his 'emporium'. John and I wandered around his shop, marvelling at the items for sale.

'Would you like to see my private collection?' the owner asked with a glint in his eye.

Housed in a room at the rear of the shop was his own bizarre collection of curious taxidermy, including animal genitalia, medical specimens, an eight-foot taxidermy Giraffe, and bones and skulls transformed into lamps.

John purchased the most beautiful crow as my Christmas present. Fashioned in mid-flight, wings spread, beady black eyes, feet clawed. Caught in that pose for all eternity.

What do you buy the woman who has everything?

It's obvious.

Taxidermy, of course!

John and I may not have been the most conventional couple but we fitted together like complimenting pieces of a unique jigsaw puzzle.

My mind still warm from that memory, I glanced around the soulless coffee shop and the people who were sharing this space, yet not connecting. I didn't care what might be going on for anyone else. I didn't care what assumptions any of these strangers might make about me: an unwashed, scruffy woman, sitting alone, no makeup, hair not done, composing notes on her phone with one finger, wearing a coat usually reserved for traipsing outdoors with the dogs.

I finished my now-lukewarm coffee and prepared to leave. Walking out into the crisp sunshine, it dawned on me: *John will be forever sixty. He won't ever be any older. He won't ever get dementia or become disabled. He won't lose his sight or go deaf. He won't lose his teeth or have a recurrence of cancer. Who knows what the future might hold for me? Maybe all of those. I don't care.*

In the past, if I'd been irritated by the annoyances of life, the kinds of things which take on exaggerated significance when nothing really bad is actually happening, I used to think I'd be fine on my own if John and I ever separated. There had even been times when I'd played with the idea of how simple day-to-day life might be if I only had myself to consider.

My Plan B had always been suicide. I'd always thought: *if life ever gets too much, if my depression ever gets too bad, I could end it.* Noone ever imagined John would take that route. Least of all me. And in so doing, he effectively denied me that path. Witnessing the devastation that death by suicide causes to those connected to the person meant I could, and would, never put anyone else through this hell.

The luxury of choice had been removed from me.

Logically, and at some deep level, I knew I would somehow be okay. I had to be. I would eventually create a new normal and live that life. Alone. Without John. But given the choice, I'd rather not have had to.

Even though I called myself an unbeliever, I now frequently implored God to reverse time so John and I could switch places. If I could have, I would have died so John could have lived. I considered all aspects of how life would be with him here and me gone. I believed the world would be a better place if things had been that way round.

The life I knew and the person I was ended with John's death. I went from being *his wife* to being *his widow*. Every time I was asked for my marital status or next of kin, my chest tightened in the vice-like grip of grief.

I am alone, I thought. *He has left me.*

32

A GLASS OR TWO OF WINE

IT WAS DECEMBER 2018, less than two months since John died. Phoebe and I had gone to London to do something for her birthday. Although the trip had seemed like a good idea, and we had tried to put on a brave face for each other, we were both utterly miserable.

Sitting in a cosy London pub with dark wooden panels and tasteful Christmas decorations, Phoebe said, 'I feel like a glass of wine.'

'If you want one, have one. Life is too short.' I shrugged.

'Will you join me?'

It was three years since I'd last had a drink. Maybe I should have followed Auntie Olive and Uncle Alb's advice and checked to see if I was too stressed. But instead, without missing a beat, I said, 'Yes, I will.'

As I waited for my wine to arrive, I wondered whether sobriety had made things harder for John. If we had continued to indulge in our nightly tipple, a smooth Cabernet Sauvignon or warm Merlot serving to lift the mood and soften strong emotions, maybe John wouldn't have needed to consult the GP.

After everything I was learning about the real effects of antidepressants, that at best they offer symptom control, was a glass of wine really that different? Maybe, when we got the news of Jim's terminal prognosis, if we were still enjoying that shared ritual, John wouldn't have taken the drugs, would never have fallen victim to their side effects, and would never have killed himself. Yet more 'what ifs' to add to all the other unanswerable questions.

Our wine arrived, we sipped and slipped into our own thoughts.

Phoebe aged about two with her Dad and uncle Jim

John was a really good dad to the boys. But Phoebe, our only daughter, had a special place in his heart. They shared interests. They liked the same kinds of music and even went to live gigs together. He's the one who accompanied her on the trip to Prague when she finally had the cosmetic surgery on her nose that she'd wanted since she was fifteen. Phoebe had lived away from home since the age of twenty-one, but came to live with us in Rainbow Cottage following the break-up of a relationship. One of the last projects John undertook was to convert our garage into a space for her dog grooming business, once again doing practical things. One of the many ways he expressed his love.

Phoebe witnessed my pain on a day-to-day basis, and I hers. We both understood, in a way noone else could, the agony of the raw gaping hole John's absence created in our existence.

Phoebe was navigating her own unique journey of loss. Our experience was not the same. But the fact we continued to live in the same home, without John, meant our grief ran in parallel. Others could perhaps more easily get on with the every day business of living, free from such constant reminders he was gone.

Autumn has always been a favourite time of year. A rich time between times. I relished the unpredictability of the fluctuating weather. Surprisingly warm sunny days, just when you think you have seen the last of them. Heavy downpours of rain replaced within minutes by blue skies and rainbows. Wild breezes sending leaves swirling to the ground creating a multicoloured squishy carpet. The chill wind signalling winter is on its way.

When I was a child, autumn was a time of Harvest Festival and Guy Fawkes night. When our children were young it included celebrations for Jake's birthday and then Halloween. We accompanied our kids and their friends trick or treating for sweets, dressed in homemade costumes and ghoulish makeup. We hosted parties where they bobbed for apples, told ghost stories, and ate party food in the dining room where John and I had covered the walls in black bin liners and fake blood. Autumn is a time of ever changing colour by day and darkness by afternoon. That wonderful, special season of mists and mellow fruitfulness.

Yet now and forever, I thought, autumn would represent something altogether different. Not the plastic skulls, white-sheet ghosts, and scary monsters of Halloween, but real horror. Real death.

Our living room was cosy, bathed in soft pools of light from mismatched lamps and the flickering glow of the log burner. In the evenings after John's death, Phoebe and I went through the motions of normality. We'd sit silently in that living room. We faced the TV rather than watched it. Neither of us having the slightest idea what was happening on the screen. We put logs on the fire. Drank cups of tea. She sat in her usual spot. I sat in mine. Next to me was an empty seat. A place where John belonged, now aching with his absence.

The mundane things, previously so comforting and enjoyable, now served merely to magnify the painful fact John was gone. Nothing was normal. Yet what else were we to do but try to engage with normal things? John wasn't there but we still occupied the same physical space, doing similar things. It is the ordinary that amplifies the extraordinary pain of loss.

Phoebe and I would sit at the same kitchen table to eat our meals. Where previously three of us had sat, now only two places were set. There was no laughter sparked by John's silly jokes. Even when we reminisced about him, trying hard to focus on all the fun, all the happiness, all the lovely times we shared, it magnified our heartache.

Phoebe and I developed a deeper love and appreciation for each other. But the jagged tear in the fabric of our lives was painfully laid bare. We were engulfed in a sometimes overwhelming combined sadness. We were living in John's home, without him, day in, day out. Others might miss him. But for us he was missing. Others might mourn his loss, but without him we felt lost.

Phoebe expressed guilt if she went out to see her friends. But sometimes I needed to be alone. At least for a while, so I could experience the full force of my grief without having to worry how it might impact her. There were times when her going out offered a respite from having to deal with her grief in addition to my own. But at other times I felt so desperately lonely I simply longed for her to return. Although noone could replace John, to have Phoebe with me offered so much comfort.

33

GRIEF IS THE THING

BEFORE JIM WAS ADMITTED to hospital for the last time, the family got together for a meal at his favourite pub. Afterwards, as we waited for the Uber outside in the dark, I gave Jim a kiss and a hug and told him I loved him. We rarely, if ever, spoke deeply or emotionally, but I am so thankful I took the opportunity that night to tell him how important he was.

Liam and his uncle Jim were close. Their relationship had deepened while Liam was at university in London. He lived in Borough Market, five minutes from Guy's Hospital, and spent a lot of time with Jim in those final weeks. I wondered if Liam treasured the opportunity to be close to and to take care of Jim because he'd been unable to do that with his dad. After all, as his twin, Jim was about as close as you could get to John.

During the eighty days that elapsed between John and Jim's deaths, I'd gone to London a few times to visit Jim. One time, Phoebe and I sneaked a bottle of red wine into his hospital room. When I opened the door to place it inside the bedside cabinet it was like a minibar in there. Apparently our idea was not unique.

'Was it because of me, Denise?' Jim wanted to know if his own impending death was responsible for John's suicide.

'I told you Jim, it was the drugs.' I reassured him as best I could. I'm not sure he believed me. The potentially lethal side effects of antidepressants are not widely publicised.

The final time I saw Jim in hospital, he was weak, his complexion grey. He seemed more than ready to go. He talked about meeting up with John in a heavenly pub.

'He'll have a bottle of Merlot ready for us to share,' Jim joked, 'And believe me, I'll give him a slap for killing himself.'

The day of Jim's funeral was crisp. The sun shone, the bright blue sky decorated by pale wisps of translucent white cloud. Mourners congregated. Each time I saw a new person I felt tears well up and the all-too-familiar tightness constricting my throat. We were there to mourn Jim, but my heart was still breaking for John. Unable to deal with waiting around for the hearse to arrive, I simply had to escape. I took myself off for a short walk. Not far from the poetically named 'St Peters and the Guardian Angels' church on Paradise Street in Bermondsey, I sat alone on a bench facing the River Thames and thought of John. Always, of course, thinking of John, and today also of Jim.

The scene before me was picturesque, like a souvenir postcard of London showing Tower Bridge and the Shard in the distance. I thought about how different the area was compared to when John and Jim were kids. How different it was even from when John and I had first met over three decades before; back then firmly a working class area. Today, trendy, gentrified, and in places very upmarket.

For a brief moment I was just a woman sitting on a bench taking in the view. I savoured this rare glimpse of normality. A brief respite from my life, which had descended so far down into madness and chaos I hardly recognised it. I took out my phone and snapped a photo of the view. I rose from the bench and returned to the church to rejoin the other mourners.

I glanced over at Ma – John's mother. Behind her stoic veneer, I saw her sadness. Losing John so suddenly, so unexpectedly, and so tragically gave me at least some insight into the pain I imagined she must be in. The loss of both her twins, just a couple of months apart, in differing circumstances, yet equally tragic, was heart-breaking. In that moment, I was struck by how the order of things was all wrong. No mother expects to outlive her children. No wife wants to be a widow. John and Jim were both such good, kind-hearted human beings. Why were they gone while others still lived?

A CELEBRATION FOR THE LIFE OF

JAMES COLLINS

13TH APRIL 1958 – 16TH JANUARY 2019

ST PETERS & THE GUARDIAN ANGELS CHURCH
PARADISE STREET
SE16

At Jim's funeral I met family members I hadn't seen since John's death. In fact, there were some I hadn't seen for many years. It made me realise how reclusive John and I had been; each other's company was all we really needed.

The juxtaposition of Jim's Catholic funeral – complete with priest, prayers, hymns, and incense – with the simple, personalised ceremony we had for John – with the shiny chrome Harley, MDF coffin we'd decorated with our artwork, and doughnuts – felt a little odd. I longed to speak about John but it was Jim's day. To me, it seemed like John's absence was the elephant in the room.

Whenever they referred to each other they'd always said, 'My brother John,' or, 'My brother Jim,' as if somehow reinforcing their bond and reminding everyone they came as a pair. On the reverse side of the order of service for the celebration of Jim's life was an old black and white photo of John and Jim when they were around six years old. They were standing on a roundabout in the play-ground at Ruskin Park, Jim smiling broadly, John squinting into the camera lens. Under the photo were the words: *Reunited, James and John.*

Re-united James and John

The church was beautiful, the service lovely. The priest, Father Michael, sensitive and just about as camp as Christmas. He recited fond memories and tributes to Jim from family members. He read what I had written about the two holidays we'd had with Jim. The first to Butlin's Bognor Regis holiday camp when the kids were little.

One day on the beach, Jim rescued a toddling little Phoebe from a big wave that threatened to engulf her. He swept her up and out of harm's way.

The second trip was many years later; Jim joined us on a vacation to Las Vegas to celebrate Liam's twenty-first birthday. We rode in a stretch limo from the airport to the hotel. Jim loved the casinos, the show girls, and having steak, eggs, and beer for breakfast in the Harley Davidson Cafe.

It was during that trip that John and I renewed our wedding vows at a little white wedding chapel. We were married by an Elvis impersonator who, we joked, looked more like David Hasselhoff than Elvis.

To all our amazement, Jim had managed to pack everything for the entire trip, including his wedding suit, into a single hand-luggage suitcase.

After Father Michael had finished recounting these stories, he looked directly at me with warmth and said, 'That was from Jim's sister-in-law, *Doreen.*'

The fact he got my name wrong, yet said it with such sincerity, was simply hilarious. Attempting as best I could to stifle what I feared others would consider inappropriate giggles, I glanced to my left. The others sharing the pew were also trying and mostly failing to suppress their laughter. As soon as we made eye contact, there was no holding back. There was an eruption of snorting giggles. It was a wonderful, joyful moment of homage to the two little boys whose childhood stories often included their mischief-making in church. I could almost see them slapping each other on the back, bent over laughing heartily at the result of this one final episode.

Only one person that day said anything to me about John's suicide. After Jim's funeral and cremation, we all gathered at his favourite pub. One of John's brothers said, 'When I heard, I was so angry. I just couldn't believe how selfish it was of John. To do that when Jim was dying of cancer.'

I tried to explain about the side effects of the prescription drugs and the research I had done, but I think he just thought I was looking for a way to excuse John or perhaps to divert blame away from myself.

A cousin, over from Ireland, asked when John's funeral would take place. I said something about the inquest taking ages and implied a funeral had not yet happened. But, of course, it already had.

Lying in bed late, as I so often did long after I awoke from whatever restless sleep I'd endured rather than enjoyed, I found myself browsing online looking for books on grief. Always looking. Always searching for something to make sense of the nonsense my life had become since John died. I came across *Grief is the Thing with Feathers,* by Max Porter.

I immediately bought the book and, as is the way of internet searches, found a link for a one-man show of the play, *Grief is the Thing with Feathers* with Cillian Murphy, Liam's favourite actor, at the Barbican in London. I decided to buy tickets for Phoebe, Liam, and Claudia too. I searched for four seats together, and for reasons I do not fully understand, the only day available was 13th

April 2019. It would have been Jim and John's sixty-first birthday. I pressed the *buy now* button.

On the day of the show, we gathered in John and Jim's sister Janice's lovely garden and raised a glass of Merlot to the twins. Father Michael attended to bless Jim's earthly remains before his ashes were buried beneath a rose tree. Jim had been a collector of baseball caps and, in tribute, we all wore one, including Father Michael. Ma poured a glass of Jim's favourite wine into the earth. They entered the world on the same day and left it just eighty days apart. Reunited in death.

Then Phoebe, Liam, Claudia, and I went to the Barbican. Cillian Murphy's performance was strange, the play dark, yet wonderful. I was enchanted. I cried.

34

ERRORS, OMISSIONS, INCONSISTENCIES

'WHAT DO I have to do to get this amended?'

I called a lawyer the minute I'd finished reading the report the police had submitted to the coroner for the inquest into John's death.

Before reading it, I'd prepared myself mentally and emotionally as best I could. I anticipated it would be difficult to be confronted by the gruesome reality, to see the details of what had happened to John in print.

What I had not been prepared for was all the mistakes and the things that were just simply untrue. To my astonishment, the report was littered with errors, omissions, and inconsistencies.

It stated John had 'previously attempted suicide by cutting his wrists'. Reading this, I was stunned. This was completely incorrect. It said John had been diagnosed with depression. Again, not true; John had never seen anyone other than the GP I'd spoken with and a relationship counsellor he'd consulted privately. He'd certainly never seen a mental health professional or received any such diagnosis. My eyes widened and my jaw dropped when I read:

John's next of kin have described how he had suffered from a long history of depression.

Why would I ever have said such a thing when it wasn't true?!

My confusion increased; apparently, we – John's family – had *noticed small things in the last few days.*

John had been tidying things up.

John had hung up his spare car keys and shown Phoebe how to use the new boiler.

I felt like everything we'd said to the police during their visit to inform us John had been killed had been totally misrepresented and taken out of context.

Yes, I'd mentioned John had tidied things up but John was always tidying things up. Yes, he'd hung up spare keys. What else does one do with spare keys? He hadn't shown Phoebe how to use the new boiler because we didn't have a new boiler. We did have a new tumble dryer and, yes, he had shown us both how it worked differently to the old one. But these things were normal and not out of character.

On the day we supposedly described these actions, we were in a state of shock, recounting the most insignificant details rather than giving accounts of reasons we believed John to be suicidal. It was as if the police had joined the dots to create the picture they expected to see when attending the home of someone who died by suicide.

Depressed people kill themselves.

If this report had been connected to a murder investigation, the errors, inconsistencies, and unfounded opinions littering it would have been considered totally unacceptable.

The driver and trainee driver of the train both gave different accounts and descriptions of John – at different points in the report!

We had been told the train that fatally struck John was empty, but the report said it had been carrying passengers.

It seemed as if attention to detail wasn't important. While the report stated that no suicide note had been found at the scene, it failed to mention that a pen and notebook *were* found in John's car, suggesting his actions were impulsive rather than planned. *As he had a notebook with him, wouldn't he have left me a note if he had planned to take his own life?*

'You don't require a solicitor if the mistakes are that obvious,' the lawyer on the phone emphasised. 'All you need to do is write a letter to the police and to the coroner. Point out the mistakes. State the report is *not a true and accurate account of events*, and state clearly how and why.'

I felt relieved; it seemed straightforward enough.

Next I called the senior police officer handling John's case.

'We can't change the report,' the detective sergeant said, sounding slightly annoyed. *Who is this mere widow who dares to question the authority of our official report?* I imagined him thinking.

Calmly but assertively I explained the details of the mistakes. His tone changed. At one point, he even mused perhaps that the officer who'd written the report had 'cut and pasted' information from another case, but he couldn't double check because that officer was away travelling.

I took issue with the egregious, sloppy approach of the police report. How could officials get these details so wrong in the face of what was really wrong: that John was dead. I was also worried that the issue of having to correct mistakes in the report might detract from more important questions, such as: What role had the side effects of the drugs played? Could John's death have been avoided? And could the inquest help prevent future deaths?

If John had been drunk or stoned when he took his life, the report would have acknowledged this as potentially significant and a likely contributing factor. Not so, with antidepressants and sleeping pills. A fact which ignores the reason that people take these drugs; because they alter the mind just like alcohol and recreational drugs do. That is their purpose. The fact they can cause serious side effects that can lead to suicide wasn't my opinion, it was fact. The only thing open to dispute is how rare these known side effects actually are.

Doctors tell patients the drugs can take two weeks to begin reducing symptoms. But from extensive research, I've learned this isn't the entire story; it's often *within* the first two weeks that the side effects kick in, which people understandably mistake for worsening symptoms of what sent them to the doctor in the first place.

I felt a burning certainty in the pit of my stomach that the inquest into John's suicide needed to at least acknowledge this.

'The report itself can't be rewritten, but if you submit the corrections and your comments in writing, that should be fine,' the DS said, not exactly admitting the police had made mistakes.

We agreed I'd submit a document to the coroner with a copy to him. He asked if I wanted to meet him on the day of the inquest, before it started. I gratefully accepted and we discussed where and when we would meet.

Following the call I went through the report, meticulously highlighting all the inaccuracies and noting, first in the margins and later typing into a document on my computer, explanations and the corresponding evidence as to why they were wrong.

I printed everything and posted it to the coroner, as well as sending a copy to the senior police officer. I retained a copy for myself. I had done all I could and had to trust it was enough to correct the record.

I was so frustrated that in the midst of grieving the loss of my husband, I was having to do this. But it was important, and it was the very least John deserved.

35

LAST MINUTE SWITCH

'JUST CHECKING that you're all still coming to the inquest tomorrow?' a coroner's officer said after I answered the phone.

'Yes,' I said, thinking, *As if I'd miss it.*

'okay. And you know where it is?'

I confirmed the address. I must have driven past Seax House, a characterless grey and glass concrete building, thousands of times, without once wondering what went on inside.

'Is there anything else I need to know before tomorrow?'

There was a pause.

I thought back to the dozens of calls I'd had with the coroner's officer over the preceding months. 'This is a big case,' he'd said during our very first call. Later, he'd said things like, 'Don't quote me on this, but I'm pretty sure the coroner will give a verdict of accidental death.'

His 'strictly off the record' comments seemed to lack professionalism, but I was hungry for evidence the coroner was genuinely interested in John's life as well as his death. I took the comments as signs the staff in the coroner's office were paying attention to the information we were passing on for consideration in the months leading up to the inquest.

'Actually there is just one thing,' he said. 'The inquest will be heard by a different coroner.'

It was as if all the air was sucked from the room and my lungs. John's inquest had already been postponed once because the coroner had a more important case to attend. For months I'd been communicating back and forth with the senior coroner for Essex. As family members, we'd been asked to submit statements of both fact and opinion on John's actions, behaviours, and state of mind prior to the suicide.

'Should we wait until nearer the inquest date and send everything in all at once?' I recalled asking.

'Oh, no. It's better to email things over as you go. That way the coroner has plenty of time to read and consider everything well in advance of the inquest.'

So that's what we'd done. Every time we emailed a family statement, the senior coroner had acknowledged receipt. And the coroner's officer had said, off the record of course, that from everything the senior coroner was reading, she was 'leaning away from suicide as a verdict' because it seemed doubtful John showed any prior intention.

Of course, I hoped that also meant the role of the prescribed drugs would be cited as a contributing factor in his death.

I'd read about other inquests into deaths where people killed themselves while under the influence of alcohol or recreational drugs, and the coroner took this into consideration. In such cases, I'd read, a verdict of suicide was often *not* given because the substances interfered with the deceased person's decision making around the actions which might result in death. Not every deliberate act resulting in death was automatically or officially considered to be suicide.

For example, a death by misadventure was where the death was primarily attributed to an accident that occurred due to a risk that was taken, either wilfully or voluntarily. So, a death caused by an overdose of recreational drugs or alcohol may be ruled 'misadventure' by a coroner. The person voluntarily took the risk of using drugs or drinking excessively which resulted in their death.

An open verdict may be recorded in a case where the coroner decided intent of the deceased could not be proven. On March 4, 2019, Senior Coroner Caroline Beasley-Murray had rendered an open verdict in the case of Keith Flint, the singer with the band The Prodigy. Even though Flint died as an apparent result of hanging himself, because he had cocaine, alcohol, and codeine in his system at the time, Beasley-Murray said that to record suicide:

"I would have to have found that, on the balance of probabilities, Mr Flint formed the idea and took a deliberate action knowing it would result in his death. Having regard to all the circumstances I don't find there's enough evidence for that. We will never quite know what was going on in his mind on that date and so that's why I'm going to record an open conclusion."[1]

---

1. Press Association. 'Keith Flint: not enough evidence for suicide verdict, coroner rules'. The Guardian, May 8, 2019. Accessed online. https://bit.ly/3xxput0

36

THE INQUEST
30TH APRIL 2019

THE DAY of the inquest had been hanging ominously on the horizon for so long I couldn't quite believe it had arrived. Preparations of our submissions for the coroner's consideration had consumed my thoughts ever since the reality of John's death sank in. Our family had been waiting for the opportunity to present the circumstances, hoping we might help save another family from going through what we had by raising awareness of the link between antidepressant medications and suicide. I could not shake the belief that the outcome of the inquest was key to providing clarity.

'It's finally struck me.' Liam's face was serious as he twiddled with the stir stick in his coffee. We were in a nearby coffee shop waiting to meet the detective sergeant before heading in to the inquest. 'Whatever happens today, it won't bring Dad back.'

There was something so final, so heartbreaking about the fact these words had been spoken aloud.

'But we've done all we can,' Liam continued. 'We've submitted family statements and raised our concerns over the drugs. As long as the coroner considers everything, the verdict itself is irrelevant.'

Verdict. The word had been used countless times during correspondence and conversation for months but suddenly it jarred. It invoked implications of being on trial for some crime.

Nothing was going to bring John back; I knew that. We all knew that. Nothing was going to make everything better. But I hoped the inquest might bring us some closure.

The policeman joined us in the coffee shop. He seemed concerned about the errors in the report.

'I still don't know what happened and until my colleague returns from her travels I can't find out.' He flipped over another page in his folder, his finger tapping a line in the middle of the page. His colleague was the coroner's enquiry coordinator for the British Transport Police.

'I did check to make sure that she hadn't confused John's case with another.' The DS shook his head and looked away. 'Unfortunately, during the inquest, I can only answer specific questions that are directly put to me. I can't offer up explanations or corrections unless I'm actually asked.'

I hoped the replacement coroner had read all the information I'd submitted about the errors, so the pertinent questions would be raised. Again I hoped I'd done enough. We packed up and headed to Seax House.

The coroner's officer I'd been speaking regularly with greeted us and showed us to the family waiting room. It was full of desks and office chairs piled up as if it was a dumping area for surplus junk from other rooms. Claudia broke the awkward silence by asking him about the variations in verdicts for cases of suicide.

'Well, let's see...' The officer puffed up, straightened his tie, and sat down. 'There was one case where the person had tied a ligature around their neck...' He proceeded to provide us with a detailed and gruesome description. He seemed to revel in the telling of the tale. There was evidence, he explained, that suggested the person had changed their mind and tried to remove it. 'But they still died, and so the verdict was not suicide.'

He droned on while I intentionally zoned out, dumbfounded at the way he was speaking to a bereaved family. In my state, I was unable to comprehend the likely desensitising impact of his line of work. I'm not sure Claudia expected what she'd gotten us into with her innocent question. Thankfully we were soon ushered into court for what we'd been told to expect would be a half-day inquest.

The assistant coroner entered the court in a whirl of pompous arrogance, her blonde hair styled like Sandy from the film *Grease*. Her girlish hairband looked strangely out of place; more suited to a teenager than a mature woman about to preside over the weighty matters surrounding the factors contributing to my husband's death. She peered over the top of half-rimmed spectacles. This replacement for the coroner I'd been communicating with for months looked like a bad actress trying to play the role of a Very Important Person, rather than actually being one.

She didn't extend sympathies to us, the family, or acknowledge that John was much loved and missed. *Was this her first inquest? Did she have a point to prove?* Was I imagining that she emitted an air of insincerity, that every word she uttered seemed a melody of the disingenuous?

The doctor who prescribed John's antidepressants was called to give evidence. He walked from the seating area with a strange limping gait which was at odds with his age. *What's wrong with him?* I wondered. *Does this have something to do with why he became a doctor?*

He swore his oath to tell the truth and began to give evidence.

Had he conducted a telephone consultation with the deceased on October 20, 2018?

Yes.

Had the patient indicated he was having trouble sleeping?

Yes.

Was he the prescribing doctor for the drugs Zopiclone and Citalopram, which the deceased had been taking at the time of death?

Yes.

Had he followed all the necessary guidelines when prescribing the drugs for the patient?

Yes.

Did he take and record notes from the consultation as he was required?

Yes.

Had he asked John any questions about his sleep hygiene?

No.

Did he feel it necessary to refer him for counselling?

No.

Finally there was a question about the side effects of the drugs. He was polite but dismissive.

Professionally, the doctor insisted, he'd done nothing wrong.

Morally, I wondered, *could the same be said?*

The assistant coroner skimmed over the subject of akathisia and other side effects of SSRIs and how these can inhibit the ability to make rational decisions. She barely referenced the drugs John was taking. To me, it appeared as if neither the prescribing doctor nor the assistant coroner had any awareness of the potential side effects of antidepressants. My fears were confirmed; it seemed like the information I had provided to raise awareness had simply been ignored. They seemed oblivious to the risk of akathisia triggering some patients to sudden, unexplained violent behaviour, including suicide and even, in some cases, murder.[1]

A creeping sense of helplessness gripped me. I wanted to scream: *No one is talking about the drugs!*

Six months previously, I'd still been an unquestioning believer in the 'chemical imbalance' myth and the harmless 'help' provided by SSRI antidepressant drugs. But now I knew differently; I knew in my heart that John's suicide was a result of the known, if 'rare', side effects of the drugs he had been prescribed.

It started to dawn on me that, as she had only been given John's case twenty-four hours before the inquest, this assistant coroner had simply not read the information provided.

Next, the DS answered questions about the CCTV footage from cameras at the train station (John on the platform, on a bench, then on the track), summaries of the witness accounts from the driver and trainee driver (not enough time to stop the train once they saw John on the track), and the distance travelled by the train before coming to a stop after impact (600 metres). All of which he answered in a calm, matter-of-fact way.

There was no mention of mistakes in the police report nor of our attempts to have the records corrected.

The assistant coroner asked for a representative of the family to take the stand. I glanced at Phoebe, Liam, and Claudia. Each nodded in agreement that it should be me.

'You said your husband had hung up his spare keys?' she asked, peering at me over her half-rims.

'Yes.'

'And that he had shown you how to use the boiler?'

'Yes.' In my anxious confusion, I'd missed my chance to point out this was one of the errors from the report.

'Do you think that was an indication he was preparing to take his own life?'

Was this some kind of joke? I looked over at my children, their expressions telling me they were as confused as I was. If she had read the statements we'd submitted, she'd know that is *not* what we believed. If she had read our statements, wouldn't she instead be asking us to explain why we believed the medications were responsible?

'With respect, we were married for thirty-two years,' I defended. 'I think if he was preparing to kill himself, John would have found more important things to focus on than his spare keys.'

She asked me something about a conversation which had supposedly taken place between John and Phoebe during the week before John died – the week I was away in London running the NLP course for Liam.

'I can't answer that because I wasn't there. But my daughter is here today.' I pointed to where Phoebe was sitting. Phoebe started to answer, but the assistant coroner cut her off.

'I only want to hear from one member of the family,' she said. I repeated that I couldn't answer her question. She dismissed me. Bewildered, I returned to my seat.

Liam had asked for the opportunity to say a few words about his dad. He'd been told by the coroner's officer it would probably be fine but that it would be up to the coroner. She refused Liam's request.

'The posters at the station, urging people to call the Samaritans if they are contemplating suicide. Are there any?' She directed this question to the DS.

'I'm afraid I don't know,' the DS glanced at us. Was I imagining the embarrassed expression on his face?

'I will write to the appropriate person,' she said with a self-satisfied flourish of her shiny silver pen.

In some ways, the inquest was set up like a court of law, but there was no opportunity for debate or discussion. I felt we had noone on our side, no representation, and no opportunity to offer opinions or thoughts, let alone challenge mistakes. Of which there were many.

After a brief adjournment, the assistant coroner returned and read out a written statement. Peering down at us over the top of her spectacles, she quoted some mumbo jumbo from another case. None of what she said meant anything to me.

She delivered her verdict: John had 'committed suicide'.

Suicide has not been a crime in the UK since 1961 when the Suicide Act was passed. That was before I was even born and John was a three-year-old toddler. *Committed* is a contentious word when used in relation to suicide, and there are campaigns to end the use of this stigmatising language. Members of Parliament, celebrities, and other campaigners say we all have a responsibility to use different language – not committed – and to think about the impact this phrase has on everyone, including bereaved families and friends.[2]

Committed suicide.

I was shocked to hear the phrase used by a professional I'd expect to know better. People *die* by suicide. They do not *commit* suicide.

With a final swish of self-importance, she was gone. The whole process, from the start of the inquest to the conclusion, had taken just over ninety minutes.

As we filed out I felt shell shocked. I had hoped that at some point during the inquest, John would have been acknowledged as a human being. But he hadn't. Far from any sense of closure, I felt even more empty. I began to realise that in expecting the authorities to do better, be more accurate, and treat us like human beings, I had failed to appreciate that everyone is fallible and filtering everything through their own subjective viewfinders. Even professionals, such as coroners, police officers, train drivers, and doctors.

We gathered outside in the lobby. The long anticipated inquest finally over, but it felt as if I was still waiting for something. I approached the doctor, his gaze fixed firmly on the ground. He managed to avoid eye contact with me until the last possible moment.

'I don't blame you personally.' I squeezed the words out between breathless sobs that robbed my lungs of air. 'There are enough victims in all this. I'm not going to add you to the list.' I could feel tears streaming down my face.

He looked right at me and in that moment I thought I detected something in his eyes. Gratitude? Sorrow? Guilt? I don't know what.

We looked at each other, two human beings oddly connected by this tragedy.

'I do blame the system you're part of. It's deeply flawed,' I said, gathering steam. 'It encourages people to believe their feelings are symptoms, that there is something wrong with them. It dishes out drugs with dangerous side effects rather than offering emotional support and reassurance that painful feelings are a normal response to tragic events. And I wish there was something that could be done to change it.'

He looked back at the ground and made no reply.

Inquests in the UK are open to the public, so anyone can attend. Two young reporters had been sitting at the back of the room. Suicide is an easy public interest story. Often bereaved families are hostile to the presence of the press. After speaking to the GP, I approached them. I could sense their discomfort.

'Here is my number and my email. If you want more information on what I believe happened, I'm willing to speak to you.'

Taking the offered paper, one of them visibly relaxed. The tension releasing from his shoulders. He gave a sigh before saying, 'Thank you. I will be in touch.'

The other also took my details and looked at me with genuine admiration. He was young, probably not yet thirty. 'I just wanted to say… you and your family showed such dignity in there.'

That started my tears all over again. Unable to speak, I tried to smile and nodded my appreciation of his kind words.

The reporters did contact me and both wrote what I considered to be sensitive and balanced pieces.[3,4] That was what we had hoped would happen at the inquest: an acknowledgement of the accepted facts, that these drugs, in some cases, can cause suicide. And that while John was distressed as a result of tragic news about his twin brother, he did not have depression and – before taking the drugs – was not suicidal.

The following morning, I again lay in bed, not wanting to face another day as a widow. I found myself scrolling through news reports of other inquest verdicts. The more I read, the more my confusion turned to anger. I just could not understand the inconsistencies in verdicts held at the same coroner's court. There appeared to be no objective criteria to decide an outcome. Instead it seemed as if it was totally up to the individual coroner to decide what they thought.

I learned with dismay that prescription drugs, including sleeping tablets and SSRIs – which are expressly intended to alter the mind –apparently *do not* have to be considered, even as contributing factors, during an inquest.

Many of those who die by suicide are taking these drugs, prescribed by general practitioners for symptoms of depression and/or anxiety. Rather than anyone considering the possibility that such drugs are *contributing factors* in these deaths, it seemed to me the drugs now were used as *evidence* the person was mentally unstable.

Incensed, I forwarded the news reports to Phoebe, Liam, and Claudia.

'What happened to us all moving on now the inquest is done with?' Claudia's words cut deep, a strong message that everyone moves through grief at their own pace and that once they have moved to a new stage, they want those around them to be over it as soon as possible too.

---

1. Neeleman, J. 'Suicide as a Crime in the UK: Legal History, International Comparisons and Present Implications'. Acta Psychiatr Scand. 1996 Oct;94(4):252-7. doi: 10.1111/j.1600-0447.1996.tb09857.x. PMID: 8911560.
2. Moss, Rachel. 'Suicide Prevention: Why We All Need to Stop Saying "Committed Suicide."' *HuffPost UK.* Accessed July 2021. https://bit.ly/3hVvMfp
3. Hawkins, Elliot. 'John Collins: Family of Tiptree Man Killed by a Train Say He Had "No Prior Intention" of Ending His Life.' *Essex Live News.* May 2, 2019. Accessed July 2021. https://bit.ly/3wszYJ6
4. Gidden, Alex. 'John Collins: Family Disagree with Inquest Verdict'. *Braintree and Witham Times.* May 8, 2019. Accessed July 2021. https://bit.ly/36sbvsA

37

IT DID NOT RAIN

29TH OCTOBER 2019

ONE YEAR AFTER DAY ZERO

FOR MUCH OF the first year after John died, I walked and talked. I showed up when and where I was supposed to and did what was expected of me. I knew I was in no fit state to see clients, so I didn't. But I fulfilled training commitments. My career as a therapist, coach, and trainer wasn't something I merely did; I'd always considered it fundamental to who I am, central to my identity. From the beginning, my work was important to our family. It provided us with more money than we ever had before. John was immensely proud of me and took every opportunity to tell people about what I did for a living.

When I gained my first degree, I felt as if I became someone. My parents highly valued education, seeing academic qualifications as evidence of intelligence. They respected people they considered to be educated. I think this was partly due to our working-class roots and partly due to the fact my parents' own schooling had been so badly disrupted by their war-time evacuations.

Having a degree meant something. The professional positions I held as a graduate, going on to become a self-employed therapist, coach, and trainer, meant something. It all meant *I was someone.* My self-worth as a human being was inextricably linked to what I did professionally.

In the early days of training to become a therapist, family members would sometimes accuse me of doing that 'therapy stuff' on them. Even when I wasn't. There were people who'd use my choice of profession as a way to criticise some aspect of my behaviour or attitude. 'I would have thought you'd know better, being a thera-pist.' It became easier to *not* be a therapist when I was off duty.

In my consulting room with a client, or standing in front of a group delivering training, I felt more *me* than at almost any other time or in any other situation. Clients and students often reported profound, life changing shifts as a result of working with me. Yet, on some level, I was playing a role, inside consumed by imposter syndrome and scared of being found out. Fear of being accused of considering myself better than others – being too big for my boots – prevented me from fully integrating my different roles into one whole. Work was the only legitimate reason not to be totally consumed by my family's needs. Maybe there were times I used it to escape.

As they got a bit older, if one of the kids was facing a choice or decision and wanted help working through options, I'd shift into professional mode and coach them. But on a day-to-day basis, I was a different me. I was not a therapist. I didn't regularly apply the knowledge I had as a professional people helper. It was sometimes easier to be non-judgmental and to practice unconditional positivity towards students and clients than with my own family.

To maintain professional confidentiality, I didn't discuss clients at home and I didn't discuss my home life with clients. It wasn't until after John died that I appreciated just how deeply embedded this separation between my work self and my home self was. His suicide and my grief at losing him broke the dam holding back all those thoughts of being a fraud and imposter. How could I help other people when I hadn't been able to help him? When I couldn't help myself?

Years earlier, a client who was having relationship problems described his marriage as a 'business arrangement' where he and his wife worked well as a team on many levels but had drifted apart emotionally. Had John thought that about us? Another client described how, on the surface, his life appeared perfect, as if he had everything anyone could want. Yet inside he felt unfulfilled and unhappy. Was that how John felt?

I thought back to a conversation we had in the fall-out after he'd disclosed his infidelities.

'Why do I have to see someone else? Can't I just talk to you? You're a therapist.'

'I might be a therapist, but I am your wife. I can't be both.'

After losing John, I was angry. But never with him. I was angry with everyone who was happy. I was angry with all the couples I saw together. All the women who still had husbands. All the stupid or horrible people in the world who were alive while John was dead. All the husbands and fathers who were still alive. All the people getting on with their ordinary lives and moaning about how hard it was. Anyone who whinged about trivial things. I felt angry, and then heartbroken, at every reference to Christmas, Father's Day, birthdays, and anniversaries.

I hated myself for being angry. And the more I hated myself the worse I felt. Even with the agony his death brought in its wake, even though he also ended my life as I knew it in the instant he ended his own, I've never felt angry with John for killing himself.

If his death was a consequence of the side effects of the drugs, which I truly believe it was, then John was a victim. He took those drugs in good faith because he thought they would make him feel better. How could I be angry with him for that?

I knew John inside out, so I know he would never have intentionally hurt me, his children, his grandchildren, his mum, or Jim. John loved me too much to purposefully inflict that kind of pain. John often put the wants and needs of those he loved before his own. And was happy to do so.

It's true I had been angry with him in the past: when he revealed his infidelity and when he worried us all so much by going AWOL for those few days. But, as a direct result of that challenging time, our love deepened, partly because we realised how much we meant to each other and partly as a result of my personal journey of introspection, which softened some of my sharper edges.

Yes, I'm angry about a lot of things. But I've never been angry with John.

I'm angry with the GP for not looking after John as he should have done. I'm angry with the pharmaceutical industry which puts profit above people. I'm angry with those who unthinkingly repeat the 'chemical imbalance' myth. I'm angry that we have been brain-washed into believing there are quick-fix solutions to life's challenges. I'm angry that we're made to believe unpleasant emotions are symptoms of illness rather than reasonable responses to painful experiences.

Not least of all, though, I'm angry at myself for not possessing the power to prevent John's death.

He was my rock. Such an overused cliche, but I often find myself thinking it. Now that John is no longer here, I'm sinking in quick-sand. The more I struggle the deeper I sink. Real life is messy and complicated and people get pissed off with each other for minor reasons. But John rarely did. He seemed to have an effortless, positive perspective most of the time, in most situations. Even when I was annoyed about something, he just got on with things and would encourage me to see a reason for gratitude.

John was a quiet man who had layers. He could be silly, impulsive, infuriating, brilliant, inventive, open minded, loving, kind. And so funny. He made me laugh every single day. I remember one day getting ready for work and telling him I had forgotten to shave my armpits. With perfect comedic timing he responded, 'Just make sure not to volunteer for anything.' When I gave him a *what-the-fuck* look, he stuck his hand up in the air like a kid who knows the answer in class and gave an exaggerated glance towards his armpit.

I miss his crazy sense of humour. I miss that feeling of laughing until your belly hurts.

John stuck by me when noone else did. He put up with all the worst aspects of who I can be. He willingly always put me first, gave me time, indulged me, considered even my most outlandish ideas. If I ever dozed off in front of the TV on the sofa, I would wake up cosy because he would always cover me with a blanket. Our relationship was uniquely perfect in its imperfection and perfectly unique – like no other.

I was twenty-three years old when we met, twenty-four, and eight months pregnant, when we married, and fifty-six-and-a-half when he died. Our lives were entwined for thirty-three years. Scrolling through photos and videos of us on my phone, it dawned on me: I had no idea how to be a grown-up without him. Much of the time I could not decide if my tears were self pity or sadness for John and what he went through. And I suppose perhaps it didn't matter. Grief and despair are complicated.

To mark the first anniversary of John's death, I wanted us – me, Liam, Claudia, and Phoebe – to be together. I wanted us to be able to comfort and support each other. I also knew I needed to be somewhere other than at home.

So I settled on a special place in Cornwall: St Nectan's Glen, the waterfall where we'd holidayed when the kids were little, and John and I had visited on our own in more recent years. A special place. A place where pagans and tourists hang ribbons of remembrance from the trees, where they carefully place little rocks into piles that appear to defy gravity and hammer coins into the trunks of fallen trees as a kind of spiritual offering.

On the long, tedious drive on October 28th at 16:52, as Phoebe drove, I wrote in the notes app on my phone: "Can't breathe. It's like a countdown clock time ticking away the remaining hours. Won't ever be able to think this time last tear he was still alive. Journey taking forever. Almost as if I still have time to save him, to stop him."

By the time we arrived at our accommodation, it was dark and raining. The place I'd booked for us was at the end of a track marked with a sign that said: UNSUITABLE FOR MOTOR VEHI-CLES. We bumped and bounced along the track, sure we had lost an exhaust pipe on the way.

We spent the evening looking through old photos, remembering past times. There was an odd atmosphere of anticipation. I didn't sleep much that night. I kept dreaming things went wrong; that it poured with rain and we missed the specific time.

I desperately needed everything to go according to plan. It felt so important, so significant that we should be at the foot of the water-fall at the precise time of the first anniversary of John's death. Liam understood and, early next morning, the two of us checked out the route so everything would go smoothly.

As we all made our way to the waterfall, a robin flew back and forth across our path, even posing for a photo. When the clock reached 10:06 a.m. on October 29th, the precise moment of the first anniversary of John's death, we stood at the foot of the waterfall holding hands. A single white feather shone bright among the fallen damp autumn leaves. We stood side by side and spoke of many things we remembered about John. We wept. We consoled each other.

In the privacy of my mind I said goodbye. I said sorry. I said thank you. I felt an overwhelming sense of love. Like the only thing he thought at the end was 'I love you'.

The only thing is love.

We were alone and had privacy until we decided it was time to move on. Then a couple of other people appeared, oblivious to the significance and beauty of our visit.

It did not rain.

Phoebe, Liam and I at the foot of St Nectan's Glen waterfall

38

THE NEXT TRAIN

WHENEVER SOMEONE DIES by suicide there are questions that will forever be unanswered. The only person who could offer some explanation, who could fill in the gaps and provide a coherent narrative, is gone.

It is impossible to be inside another person's head. Noone can know another person's thoughts or walk in their shoes. But we can make an informed best guess. We can look at the facts, consider relevant information, and pay attention to the accounts of those who've had similar experiences.

What follows is a possibility, a product of my creative imagination based upon my knowledge of John, reflection on the available first-person accounts, and the information I discovered about the side effects of the drugs he was prescribed. I do not pretend this is what happened. It is merely a possibility.

39

THE NEXT TRAIN AT PLATFORM TWO DOES NOT STOP HERE.

FEELINGS OF CONFUSION and agitation were building inside John like a storm across a darkening sky. He drove, for all intents and purposes appearing fully present. But his mind was somewhere else entirely. Familiar roads and landmarks rushed past – unseen.

Instead, in John's mind's eye flashed snapshots of disjointed images and memories, one after the other. Images of his brother Jim popped up into consciousness as if from nowhere. Images and memories, both recent and from way back.

John remembered himself and Jim, the twins, two skinny little boys dressed the same, one with thick glasses. He remembered a trip to Ruskin Park feeding the ducks. Playing in the playground. Spinning faster and faster and faster on the roundabout. Chasing each other up the ladder before jumping down the slide. Competing to see who could go the highest on the swings. The feeling of being little and pushed and shoved in the crowd at East Street market. The sweet taste of a warm sarsaparilla drink on a cold winter day. A clear image of the dark kitchen in their home in New Church Road. Did he remember? Or was it that Ma had told him how, when they were just toddlers, John had climbed up on the kitchen cupboard to get the biscuit tin?

'I'll get you a biccy, Jim,' John said to his brother, who sat on the floor squinting expectantly at his twin.

The car felt to John as if it was on automatic pilot, in charge of choosing the destination and driving itself. He became suddenly restless and claustrophobic. He fidgeted, feeling uncomfortable in the usually comfortable driver's seat. It was like he couldn't bear to sit still, even while driving. John blinked and rubbed his eyes, trying to clear his blurred vision in order to concentrate on the road ahead.

Flashbacks of drunken teenage nights out in Bermondsey. Of jokes and laughter. His trip to Israel to live on the Kibbutz.

He was so tired. Every fibre of his being was exhausted. Yet he knew for certain that even if, right now, he was at home in the comfort of his own bed, sleep would evade him.

Where am I supposed to be going? What am I supposed to be doing?

A clear memory of the time Ma had taken all the kids on the bus, in the darkness of a December afternoon, to see Santa. The Christmas illuminations along Oxford Street, twinkling high above them like beautiful stars. Jim had started to cry when the visit was over because he forgot to tell Santa he had been a good boy.

The car slowed to a stop and John flicked the indicator to turn right, the tic-tic-tic sound was strangely hypnotic.

Disjointed memories of school and church continued to pop up in a random order. John smiled as he remembered pulling faces at Jim as they sat together in church. Every time the priest looked away from the congregation and down at the lectern, John would make another face to make Jim giggle.

An image of the two of them as young men, cycling in the early morning over Tower Bridge towards the sandwich shop where they both worked. Then an image of Jim ordering steak, eggs, and beer for breakfast in the Harley Davidson Cafe when they went to Vegas.

Suddenly a loud car horn shattered the memory into shards, which flew around the interior of the car and hit John hard in the chest. He nearly jumped out of his skin. His heart raced. He shouted and gestured in an uncharacteristically aggressive way at the driver in the car behind, who still sounded their horn.

In truth, John had no idea how long he had been siting there, indicating to turn, the car stationary. His mind elsewhere.

Where am I supposed to be going? What am I supposed to be doing?

As the car pulled into a space in the station car park, John saw another image of Jim. This time it was bang up to date. Beneath the signature baseball cap, his crazy curly hair all gone, his head now bald from the effects of the chemo. John looked up and out of the windscreen and for a moment was unsure where exactly he was.

What am I supposed to be doing? Where am I supposed to be going?

Looking around at the other parked cars and the platform, he realised he was at Kelvedon train station. Again.

He'd been here on the fifteenth and again just two days ago to catch a train to London to go see Jim.

What am I doing here now?

His thoughts were muddled. A pang of anger towards himself shot through his system.

What's the matter with me? Am I going mad? Why can't I remember the reason I'm here? Where am I supposed to be going? What am I supposed to be doing?

In a sudden outburst, he slapped the side of his head with the palm of his hand. Once, twice, as if trying to get the thoughts back in order.

Am I supposed to be catching a train to London? Does Jim have a hospital appointment? Was that today?

He glanced in the direction of the passenger seat and noticed his work diary lying open.

Am I supposed to be working? Do I have appointments today? Is there a customer right at this very moment expecting me?

Why can't I think straight?

Where am I supposed to be going? What am I supposed to be doing?

In that moment he felt like such a failure. Jim was the one dying of cancer and here he was unable to think straight. A powerful, painful thought flashed through his mind: *Everyone would be so much better off without me. Maybe I should be the one to die?*

An image of Denise looking at him, a concerned frown across her face. She was telling him to come back, to get some rest, to spend the day with her at home.

Am I supposed to be with her?

Where am I supposed to be going? What am I supposed to be doing?

He had to get out of the car. He had to move. He couldn't keep still. It was as if his very skin was crawling. He saw the ticket machine and moved towards it.

He must be going to London.

Why else would I be here?

Fumbling with the coins, he inserted enough money into the machine to pay for all day parking. If he was going to London he would need to pay for the whole day.

It felt a little better to be out in the air, moving. Swiftly he walked back to the car and placed the ticket on the dashboard. As he closed the car door, he checked the ticket was still clearly visible. He'd been caught before, when the burst of air from the closing car door made the ticket flip over and he got a parking fine because the ticket was not visible. How come he could remember that?

Where am I supposed to be going? What am I supposed to be doing?

Zipping up his jacket, he stuffed his hands into his pockets and walked purposefully towards the entrance to the platform.

The station was empty. There was no-one else there.

Why is the station empty?

What time is it?

Am I supposed to be going to London?

Why can't I think straight?

Irritation, anxiety, and anger competed for supremacy within his mind and body. Gnawing anxiety made his heart pound painfully hard and fast. John was afraid he was losing his mind, unable to remember what he was supposed to be doing or where he was supposed to be going.

An incessant ringing in his ears seemed to be getting louder. Interrupting his ability to think straight. He had learned to accept tinnitus as something he just had to live with, but this? Louder and louder; a deafening torture which threatened to drown out even his own thoughts. He shook his head as if trying to fling the ringing noise out of his ears, out of his head. It reminded him of shaking his head to get water out of his ears after swimming.

He walked towards the pedestrian bridge that crossed the train tracks. If he was going to London he needed to be on the other platform. But… was he going to London?

A creeping sense that he was in the wrong place came over him. Something did not seem right. Like being in a dream where things are almost normal, almost as they should be. But not quite.

Where am I supposed to be going? What am I supposed to be doing?

He was becoming irritable and impatient. Why was he acting like such an idiot? Another flashback popped into his mind. He saw Denise in their bedroom at the house in Crescent Rd, Chelmsford, years before. She was looking at him and smiling.

'Why do you act like such an idiot?'

'What makes you think I'm acting?'

They howled with laughter.

Maybe I should go home?

But then, suppose Jim is expecting me?

Nearing the pedestrian bridge to the opposite platform, John paused. Still feeling confused, unsure.

Am I supposed to be getting the train to London?

Is that why I am here?

Or am I supposed to be somewhere else?

He'd been taking the medication the doctor gave him. It was supposed to help. Why was he still not sleeping? Why was he still feeling so awful? Worse in fact. Everyone said it would make him feel better but he felt worse.

If I feel this terrible on the medication, how will I ever be able to cope without it?

What's happening?

If only I could sleep.

Maybe I'll sleep on the train.

But what if I miss the stop?

No, it's okay. Liverpool Street Station is the last stop.

Or should I get off the train at Stratford and get the Jubilee line? Yes that's it.

So should I sleep on the train or not?

If only the raging, gripping pain of anxiety, the palpitations in his chest, and the churning in his stomach would stop.

He still wasn't convinced he was supposed to be here.

What's happening to me?

Where am I supposed to be going? What am I supposed to be doing?

The station speakers burst into life.

THE NEXT TRAIN AT PLATFORM TWO DOES NOT STOP HERE. STAND CLEAR OF THE PLATFORM EDGE. FAST TRAIN APPROACHING. FOR YOUR OWN SAFETY YOU ARE REMINDED TO STAND BEHIND THE YELLOW LINE.

John felt the whoosh of the through-train creating a vacuum. He took a step back from the edge of the platform and closed his eyes until the thundering monster passed.

I just need to think.

He paused, then walked back along the platform the way he had just come. He continued to walk in the direction of the car park.

Maybe I'll go home.

At the last bench on the platform, he sat down.

I'll just sit for a moment. Gather my thoughts. Work out what's going on and what I should do.

Maybe I'll remember…

Where I am supposed to be? Where am I supposed to be going? What am I supposed to be doing?

The bench was hard and uncomfortable. He didn't really want to stop moving. But where should he move to?

Pulling his phone from his pocket, he thought maybe he should check if he had already bought a ticket. But then, staring at the screen, he forgot why he was looking at it.

Why am I here?

What's happening?

What's going on?

The announcement made him jump. THE NEXT TRAIN AT PLATFORM TWO DOES NOT STOP HERE.

Stop. Here.

Stop.

Just need this to stop.

Here.

Just for a moment.

Just need this feeling to stop now.

John glanced to the right along the track. The train was approaching fast. Still in the distance but nearly there.

What would it be like for everything to just stop here?

40

DEAR JOHN

Do you remember 'it's time to celebrate'? You used to sing the jingle from that TV advert. Usually as you came through the front door after work, holding aloft a bottle or two of our favourite red wine. That silly grin, that comic expression, saying 'Is it too early?' You and I had many reasons to celebrate over the years. We had hard times. But we also had lovely times, happy times and funny times too.

You were a good man. Simple in your tastes. Humble in your achievements and talents. And so much fun to be with.

Do you remember the day we went to the bank and paid the final instalment of the mortgage? What a monumental success that was for us. To have actually bought and paid for our very own home. To be bonafide home owners! Us! Do you remember how much we laughed because you expected there to be some kind of celebration at the bank when we did it. You were expecting an explosion of streamers and balloons and an accompanying fanfare. Or, at the very least a handshake from the manager. Instead the lady at the counter simply took the payment and handed you the receipt. Your face was a picture. We had our own celebration, though. Remember the big gold and black card I bought that said 'Congratulations! You did it!'

I miss you so much John. You are the only person who shares my history. The only person I could reminisce with who also remembers all this stuff. And now you're gone. And there is this gaping great space in my heart that is YOU shaped.

41

'DEPRESSION AND ANXIETY ARE DESCRIPTIONS, THEY ARE NOT MEDICAL DIAGNOSES.'

THE RAIN MADE it tricky to know what lane I was supposed to be in on this unfamiliar one way system in this unfamiliar town. The sat nav announced, in its self-satisfied voice, that I'd reached my destination, but I clearly hadn't. I peered through the windscreen, scanning the strange location in search of a sign. My heart beat hard and fast. Anxiety rose from my chest to my head, muddling my thoughts even more.

It was December 2019. Fourteen months after John died. I was en route to the twentieth AD4E event.

A Disorder for Everyone.

A movement challenging the culture of psychiatric diagnosis. When I'd first enquired I was told it was sold out, so I contacted the organiser and editor of *Drop the Disorder* – a book of lived experience stories from mental health survivors and contributions from highly regarded professionals. After telling her about what happened to John and why I wanted to attend, she kindly made a ticket available.

Finally I spotted a sign. The car park wasn't my intended destination but it would do. After parking the car I started walking. Staring at Google Maps on my phone I squinted through the lashing rain trying to work out which direction I was supposed to take. I felt flustered and unprepared.

Rummaging through my bag, to my dismay I realised I'd forgotten my umbrella. The rest of the journey I alternated between being hot and sweaty when I put my coat hood up and soaked through when I put it down. After a few wrong turns, I eventually found the venue. Entering the converted church with its high exposed beams and big windows, I breathed a silent sigh of relief.

Although I'd gotten all stressed about being late, there were still a few minutes before the conference was due to start. It occurred to me that before I'd lost John, I'd have been so much more laid back. Travelling to an unfamiliar town, even the thought of being late, simply wouldn't have phased me. Now, everything seemed just that bit more difficult. I worried more and felt less able to cope with even minor stressors.

The main speaker headlining the AD4E event was James Davies, co-founder of CEP and author of *Cracked: The Unhappy Truth About Psychiatry*. I'd read the book, wide-eyed, with incredulity at what it contained. Everything Davies wrote made so much sense. I was astonished and infuriated that the information he revealed wasn't common knowledge. His book led me to many other sources of information, and I was eager to hear him speak and perhaps have the opportunity to meet him. Just before his scheduled slot, it was announced he was unable to attend. My heart sank. I shook it off and vowed to get as much as I could from the event.

The day turned out to be fascinating. One of the speakers was Dr Sami Timimi, NHS consultant psychiatrist and a visiting professor of child psychiatry and mental health improvement at the University of Lincoln, UK. Speaking in a soft yet authoritative voice he said something that made complete sense of all the nonsense I had been struggling with since John died.

"Depression and anxiety are descriptions. They are not medical diagnosis. Saying you are depressed because you have depression is like saying you have a pain in your head because you have a headache."
Dr Sami Timimi, NHS Consultant Psychiatrist

I'd lived my life burdened by deep melancholy and anxiety which I had no idea how to shift. I'd been sad and scared and, like my mum before me, ill-equipped to know how to change. From an early age my heart had been emotionally calcified, a process exacerbated by experiences and actually compounded by the emotional blunting effect of the SSRI drugs I had taken for years as a *treatment* for my 'depression'.

'Depression is something you do, not something you have.'

I'd heard this before from the tutor on my hypnotherapy diploma, from Tony Robbins, but back then I wasn't ready to *hear* it.

Had I felt depressed? Yes, of course I had.

Had I experienced psychological distress? Yes, on more than one occasion.

But did I *have* this thing called depression, created by some sort of malfunction in my brain? No. I now no longer believed the myth.

Now I was sure there wasn't anything fundamentally wrong with me. And it wasn't my fault, although I had felt, at some level and for most of my life, like I was to blame for my so-called depression. It wasn't anyone's fault.

And there had been nothing fundamentally wrong with John.

John undoubtedly had *feelings* of depression and anxiety at the prospect of losing his twin to cancer. But he did not have a medical condition requiring mind-altering drugs. I was more convinced than ever that John was a victim of the side effects of drugs too readily handed out to people experiencing normal, painful, psychological responses to challenging life events.

In another presentation, Professor Dr John Read likened the current mental health system to witch hunting. In medieval times, any unfortunate woman accused of witchcraft was subjected to a trial by water. When submerged, floating to the surface confirmed her guilt and she faced burning at the stake. The only proof of innocence was death by drowning. Today, if you are prescribed a drug that makes you crazy, the craziness caused by the drug is used as proof you're crazy enough to need the drug.

The words of the GP who prescribed John the drugs came back to me: *'Depressed people kill themselves.'*

No further investigation or explanation required. If someone taking an antidepressant dies by suicide, the very fact they were prescribed the drug is regarded as sufficient proof they were mentally unstable enough to take their own life. The drug is exonerated. Any consideration of how the drug may have contributed is dismissed.

42

I HAD THIS REALLY VIVID DREAM

THERE WAS a group of people on a pirate ship. Not a real one, more like the kind found at a theme park. The night sky blended into the surrounding still water, inky black and impenetrable. Raucous, boisterous, and cajoling voices dared someone to dive into the water and retrieve a key. The person being dared protested he couldn't swim. Although not falling-down drunk, he'd clearly been drinking. The rowdy teasing increased in volume and instance. Giving in to the mounting pressure, the inebriated person finally leapt clumsily from the deck of the ship and disappeared beneath the surface of the dark water.

In my dream, the morning after, when the person had sobered up and his brain was back to normal functioning, free from the psychoactive effects of the alcohol, he was shaking his head in disbelief. 'My God, what was I thinking? Why did I do that?'

This dream reinforced for me how behaviour is influenced by psychoactive substances, which alter perceptions and impair the ability to make informed, rational decisions. People become impulsive and do things they wouldn't do otherwise. The substance in the case of the person in my dream was alcohol. For John, it was a prescribed antidepressant.

I know there have always been people who experience mental illness. But I reflected on how we've been encouraged to talk about mental health rather than mental illness. It's a good thing to talk about more openly, but is it encouraging too many of us to self-diagnose and eagerly ask our doctors for the pills we believe are a miracle solution?

I was seeing antidepressants in a different light. What if the message changed? How would we react if told we had a mental illness requiring powerful mind-altering psychiatric drugs, which have an array of side effects ranging from mildly unpleasant to potentially life threatening? Would we regard their prescription as quite so harmless?

Antidepressants do work for some people, of course. But I was finding a lot of evidence and information that they do not work for many others. And they work significantly less well when no counselling accompanies the medication. Which, based on my experience, John's experience, and the experiences others have told me about, is what happens most of the time.

Perhaps John's death was avoidable. If he'd not been prescribed the drugs, I don't think his distress would have led to suicide. He wasn't mentally ill – his medical records confirmed there had never been any such diagnosis. The records show he'd consulted GPs only eight times during a period of twenty-four years to talk about feeling anxious. On none of those eight occasions did the GP think John's discomfort was serious enough to warrant referral for any kind of mental health assessment, to any mental health specialist, or to any therapy or counselling.

John's death was a symptom of what I began to see as a much broader problem: a widespread collective unwillingness to tolerate any sort of unpleasant emotion.

Somehow, we have been led to believe our painful emotions are symptoms of a mental health problem, the treatment for which is a prescription.

43

SOBS

As I ENTERED the church hall on a dark Wednesday evening, I didn't know what to expect and felt nervous. It was my first time at the meeting for survivors of bereavement by suicide – SOBS, an acronym I found uncomfortably sentimental. Their website says the group does not offer counselling but rather has a focus on self-help. Through sharing experiences, the idea is we can connect, break our isolation, and support each other.

Looking around the hall, I was surprised how many people were present. About forty of us, some sitting quietly, some chatting, some scanning the scene like me, a little uncertain. There was a broad mixture of men and women of all ages. We were all different, yet we had at least one thing in common. And each of us was sufficiently motivated to leave the relative comfort of our own homes to gather together in search of the support of strangers who, perhaps, understood what it was like to be bereaved by suicide.

Once the meeting formally began, one by one each person revealed their story. Each one heartbreakingly tragic and unique. Not one of them like John's. My fellow bereaved spoke about their loved ones as people who had tried multiple times to take their own lives, as people with documented histories of mental illness, people well known to crisis teams, mental health services, and the police. They described repeated admissions to hospital, both voluntary and sectioned under the Mental Health Act, either for their own or others' safety. Some even described a sense of relief when their loved one finally succeeded in completing the act, the black cloud of fear they'd lived beneath for so long transformed into a thunderstorm of grief.

How many of the people who had died were taking antidepressants? I wondered.

I listened intently but didn't speak during the meeting. I was too exhausted by the telling of the tale. And I didn't know how to position John's death amongst all these stories of the lengthy mental torment of their loved ones.

My gaze slid from one face to another, a shared sadness connecting everyone in that room and every person they grieved for. It hung between us, ensnaring us like invisible threads of a sticky spider web.

44

OIL AND WATER

IT'S TEMPTING to imagine that the devastating trauma of losing a husband, a father, suddenly and unexpectedly to suicide, might bring the bereaved closer together. Sadly this is not always the case. Liam and Claudia became distant. Liam did what sons are prone to do; he integrated closer into his wife's family. Daughters often stay close to their mums and their husbands follow.

Liam and Claudia understandably wished to put all the sadness behind them. Their focus was firmly on the future, and the baby Claudia had talked about for so long. I was happy *for* them, but it was hard for me to wholeheartedly celebrate. They had a wonderful new beginning to look forward to; becoming parents.

Unfortunately their happiness at this new phase in their lives could not make me less unhappy about the endings I was coming to terms with. In fact, on one level, learning there was to be a new grandchild served to emphasise the reality of everything and everyone I'd lost. I was deeply sad John would never meet this grandchild or be a living part of their life.

Rather like different shades of pain that could merge and transform, their happiness and my unhappiness reacted like oil and water. Liam and Claudia said I was selfish and negative and lacked consideration. Maybe they were right, but it was not deliberate. If I could have been different, I would have been. They said, 'Don't stomp all over our happiness just because you're unhappy.'

That had not been my intention, and I felt woefully misunderstood. 'If you can't be genuinely happy for us, maybe it's best we don't speak until you have worked through whatever is creating these negative feelings.'

I tried but failed to make them understand that my 'negative feelings' had nothing to do with them. I was still grieving. My feelings were the result of losing John and the life we had.

The professional knowledge I have as a therapist, coach, and trainer, which helped me support others with their loss, did nothing for me as a person navigating the uncharted ocean of widowhood. It wasn't Denise the therapist who lost John. It was Denise the wife.

I had no idea what to do with these feelings. I had no box to conveniently pack them into. How could I begin to explain to Liam and Claudia that, for me, the future was an uninviting place? That the present moment was something I endured? How could I explain that the only thing I truly wanted was a return to the past?

As Phoebe and I both felt more and more excluded from Liam and Claudia's life, the resulting feelings of rejection, of even more loss, were painful. I remain hopeful that one day things will be okay between us. But at the moment I feel stuck between a rock and a hard place, as if whatever I do or don't do will in some way make things worse. Damned if I do and damned if I don't. I recognise my feelings are a barrier to moving on but, for now, because I really have no idea what to do to make things right, I've decided to pause, to wait, and to take no action. Sadly, this breakdown in our relationship coincided with the fall out from the global pandemic.

When it became impossible to ignore the reality of just how serious Covid-19 was, most people were thrown into a spiral of anxiety. Restrictions put a stop to almost every aspect of normal life suddenly and unexpectedly. We were instructed to stay at home, alone. Elements of life which had previously seemed so certain were now totally unpredictable. Lockdown left people feeling powerless and vulnerable.

The impact of all this illustrated the true fragility of life and how close death always is. It emphasised how little control anyone actually has. In some ways I felt as if the rest of the world had access to how I felt as a result of losing John; normal life ended, feelings of fear, isolation and sadness overwhelmed, no aspect of existence was left unscathed by the realisation of how unstable life is.

Fear, loss and loneliness infected every aspect of existence.

45

REASONS TO LIVE

I READ SOMEWHERE that those bereaved by suicide are at a higher risk of killing themselves. I understand this completely. Some days the thought *I do not want to carry on living* will take me by surprise. Feelings of regret, sadness, and guilt threaten to drag me to a place I am fearful of going. I dwell on painful past events, some of which were my fault, some beyond my control, and I wonder: *If I kill myself, would anyone really care?*

Some mornings I feel as if the only reason I get out of bed is because Doug and the other dogs need me. Never could I have imagined a reason to live would come down to something as ludicrous as four old rescue dogs wanting their morning walk.

I also read that one reason antidepressants push people from distressed to acting on suicidal thoughts is the emotional blunting effect. The pills literally inhibit the ability to appreciate the feelings of others. The person can no longer imagine or relate to the devastation their death would cause. It's not because of their mental health problem, it's a cruel and insidious side effect. The drug robs them of empathy.

What prevents me from ending my life on my darkest days is of course more than four old rescue dogs. Although I can't imagine who else would care for them if I wasn't here. What stops me is the knowledge of what it would do to Phoebe. I love her so deeply I would endure any pain myself to prevent her from suffering.

The antidepressant pills I had diligently taken every day for so long, now remained untouched in the bathroom cabinet. Immediately following the discoveries I made about the myth of the chemical imbalance, and the side effects so many people like John experience, I stopped taking them. At the time in my life when arguably I should have needed them more than ever, I went cold turkey. Due to the state of grief I was experiencing, it is impossible to assess what impact withdrawal had on me. Sudden unexpected death, such as John's, complicates grief to the point that some believe it creates a kind of post traumatic stress. Although in reality the stress is anything but post. I certainly know that I felt brain zaps - electric shocks striking like bolts of lightening through my brain. These are recognised as one of the effects of withdrawal from antidepressants.

46

AS FAR AS THE EYE CAN SEE

THE TWO-DAY RETREAT promised time and space to consider where you are in life and where you might choose to go next. Something deep inside told me it would be useful.

In spite of setting off at 7:00 am, a journey that should have taken under two hours took me three and a half, due to traffic holdups which were in turn due to the lashing rain.

The retreat, although non-religious, took place within a Christian centre. A beautiful house in beautiful grounds. We were treated to lots of tea, coffee, and plenty of cake. We enjoyed fresh home grown vegetables at each home cooked meal. The house, spotlessly clean yet homely and welcoming, had once been a country retreat for a well-to-do family. The house and the grounds on which it sat emanated a spirit of warmth and regenerative rest. The retreat guides were jolly, kind, and non-directive, my fellow participants nice enough strangers on the journey we embarked upon together.

After a comfortable first night and pleasantly nourished from the lovely breakfast, I took my coffee to the training room. Soaking up the warmth of the atmosphere, I settled into one of the armchairs, looking forward to being snug and cozy inside for the day.

My heart sank when the retreat guide said the first exercise of the morning involved going outside. I glanced out of one of the huge rectangular sash windows. The drizzle and wind made even the beautiful autumnal landscape unappealing. It was Oxfordshire. In November. Of course it was raining.

I took my time preparing for the walk, as if it was some mammoth expedition. I dilly-dallied getting my boots on. I didn't rush going to the loo or getting into my winter coat. I didn't want to be cold but, more than that, I didn't believe I'd get much from the activity. After all, at home I walked every day. Having dogs meant it was sometimes a choice made for me.

Being away on retreat was supposed to be a bit of a rest from having to go outside in all weathers. After John died, I walked every day on heathland close to where we lived. I walked mindfully, paying attention to my breath, to everything on purpose and without judgement. I did not want to do it here on retreat. When I couldn't think of any more ways to delay the inevitable, I exited the warmth of the house through the big front door.

The instruction was to walk and use all our senses to be aware of what emerged. My delaying tactics had already cut into the twenty-five-minute exercise by almost ten minutes. Pulling up my hood, I crunched across the gravel drive, passing the field with the sheep, and headed towards an avenue of tall trees. In the distance I spotted one of my fellow retreat attendees, a funny character who had been some kind of minister in a previous life. Not wanting to risk having to engage in polite small talk, I pretended not to see him and walked in the opposite direction.

The beautiful mix of swirling grey, blue, and violet clouds moving fast across the low sky transported my mind somewhere else. Remembering the instruction for the exercise, I pulled my mind back to where I was.

Even through the drizzle, an array of rich autumn colours splashed against one another. Red, yellow, and orange leaves. Brown mud patches. The patchy faded green of the grass. The yellowy brown of windfall apples strewn across the ground. My huffing and puffing breath. The crunch of my boots on the ground. The rustling of my clothes. A wayward toggle clinking with the rhythm of my every step as it knocked against the zipper of my coat.

Still, I resisted. I did not want to be outside. I did not want to be walking. The rain temporarily stopped. I reached out and ran a finger over the surface of a wooden bench, one of several strategically placed here and there in the grounds. As I suspected, it was very wet. The kind of wet that is deeply ingrained. The kind of wet that might feel okay at first if you perch just on the edge of the seat. But the kind of wet that will seep through layers of outside clothing, right down to the skin, leading to the enduring experience of a damp backside for the rest of the day.

Reluctantly, I continued on with my walk, wondering if it was time to go back yet.

Not far in front of me, I spied a little wooden summerhouse. Painted a jolly shade of blue, it faced hills and overlapping fields in various shades of autumn post-harvest. I decided to explore. Peering through the window to look inside, I saw it was at least dry. If I went in, I'd still technically be exploring the outside, wouldn't I?

Reaching out, I tried the door handle, half expecting it would be locked up, sleeping, waiting for the beginning of springtime. It was open. I went inside and sat on the little sofa. There were candles and a crucifix on a wooden stand. A mirror that had a quote written in white permanent marker which I couldn't quite read.

Sitting in solitude, I gazed outside, my eyes scanning the scene. From this vantage point it was possible to see a long, long way into the distance. Fields, trees, sky, mist, on and on.

A pair of red kite birds glided, circled, and swooped above the tall treetops. Much closer, a smaller bird propelled itself gracefully through the sky. Flapping its wings wildly, flap, flap, flap, flap. Then tucking its wings in close to its body. Presumably to rest for a second or two from the effort of flying. It dropped rapidly in midair before flapping again. Flap, flap, flap, flap. Repeating the process, propelling itself to wherever it was going.

Do birds always have a purpose? A reason to fly somewhere? Or do they just sometimes fly simply because they can?

Softening my gaze without realising what I was doing, I took in the whole scene.

The phrase *as far as the eye can see* popped into my head. I was literally looking as far as the eye can see.

Then it came to me. No matter how far *as far as the eye can see* actually is, you can't see everything there is. Beyond, in the distance, I knew there were roads and buildings and people. But from where I sat, I couldn't actually see them. Even though I couldn't see them, they still existed.

As far as the eye can see is only as far as the eye can see from your current vantage point. And if you didn't know better, it would be really easy to believe that what you see is all there is. From where I sat, if I didn't know any different, it would have been easy to think this was the entire world. All of existence. After all, I could see a very long way.

Since John died, there had been lots of signs that, if I had believed in a life beyond death, I would have taken as comforting proof. But I was adamant in my belief that there was nothing, so I dismissed them all.

A hummingbird. A Harley. A purple Vegas casino chip.

If the question ever came up, 'What do you think it's like after you die?' John would respond with, 'Just like it was before you were born.'

In many ways, I prided myself on being an open-minded person. An I'll-believe-it-if-I-see-it kind of person. But an uncomfortable truth was dawning on me; I was not as open-minded as I'd thought.

I could behave in quite a dismissive, even superior, way towards those who believe in such nonsense as the existence of life after death. The truth was that since John died, even when I saw signs, I did not choose to believe, instead dismissing them as mere coincidence. As simply my own sad desire or need for some kind of comfort. As if that was a bad thing. A weak, feeble-minded kind of thing.

I stopped noticing the rain that had sneakily recommenced and instead absorbed this miraculous autumn day. My mind wandered to consider the word *sign*. I thought about road signs: road ahead closed, warning, slow down, one way, accident ahead. Information signs; signs you could notice or not. You could pay heed or ignore. You could comprehend or misunderstand.

Signs are merely an abstraction that illustrate certain elements of a larger, more complex reality. Signs as just that. Signs. Combine all that with the fact human beings are story tellers and meaning makers. We simply cannot help but interpret what we see based on what we already believe or have direct experience of – and the infinite nature of possibility begins to emerge.

Was life really as random as I always professed?

Was life really as meaningless?

Life is shit and then you die and then there is nothing. Really?

Life is mostly just dealing with stuff on a day-to-day basis. Or is it?

Life is mostly a mediocre existence punctuated by brief intense moments of joy, and bliss, and misery, and fear. Really?

Shifting to shake off the discomfort of such thoughts, I considered the Christians at the retreat house. They seemed so at peace. Content. Not high-fiving bundles of awesomeness but quietly *happy*. Was I envious of their abiding faith in something?

When I was about ten or eleven, I told my parents I was going to church. I went with a neighbour, Mrs Watson, a nice lady who grew beautiful flowers. But after that one time, I never went again. Whatever I was looking for, I didn't find it at the Denmark Hill Baptist Church in Camberwell.

My mum and dad had both my sister and I baptised when we were babies. My mum explained that being baptised was like having insurance, the spiritual equivalent to making sure you always have an umbrella in your bag. *Just in case.*

I always thought it seemed odd, given my dad had no religious beliefs whatsoever and my mum… well, Mum did refer to God on occasion but not in a way that implied she had any kind of really close relationship with Him. Or Her.

That day, in that moment, looking out over the Oxfordshire countryside through the mist of fine drizzly rain, I made a decision. A surprising decision. That I *do* have faith.

Faith that there is more than just *as far as the eye can see.*

Faith that there is another field beyond the field I can see from here.

Faith that the nature of *that field* is unknowable to us here in *this field*.

Everything in this field is *of this field*. The field beyond, because it is beyond, is unknowable to us here in this field. That is the order of things. That is as things should be. Those who profess to know or have access to *that field* are either wilfully taking advantage of those who wish for confirmation *that field* exists or they're delusional.

I decided to engage with the signs. To welcome them and to know I could choose to take comfort from them. To believe that John is somewhere better. Somewhere at present unknowable to me because I am in *this field*.

Because why would I *not* choose to believe that?

Beliefs are strongly held opinions. By virtue of their nature, beliefs cannot be proven because they are not facts. In effect we can choose to believe whatever we want to. So, again, sitting in that little summerhouse I asked myself: *Why would I not choose to believe that John is in another field called, for example, heaven?* Whatever that means, or wherever that is, isn't relevant.

Glancing at my watch I saw it was time to return.

As I made my way back toward the glowing, warm comfort of the main house, I took a step and felt my foot sink into the flesh of a soft, damp, fallen apple. It drew my attention to the ground. Among all the shades of golden leaves, there were dozens of fallen apples. Some almost whole yet bruised. Some broken or half-eaten. Their mushy flesh dappled brown. We had been told that if so moved, we should bring something back with us. I looked at the apples and wondered about taking one back and making something up about the cycle of life and death. But instead I decided each apple was perfectly placed exactly where it was. Who was I to move any of them? It felt so much more meaningful to leave them where they were. It symbolised the idea that everything was somehow exactly where it should be, playing its part in the cycle of life. Not tidy. Not pretty. Not particularly nice. But somehow as it needed to be.

I may still choose not to describe myself as spiritual, but I do have hope. Hope that even when you can see as far as the eye can see, more does exist. You just can't see it from where you are.

47

A HOLE IN THE ROOF

THERE WAS water on the floor. A big puddle. In the living room, just in front of the log burner. I eyed Doug with suspicion as he snoozed on the sofa. As if sensing he was being silently accused, he lifted his head and gazed right at me. He had a nothing-to-do-with-me expression. I swear, if dogs could shrug their shoulders, he would have.

On closer inspection, the pool of water was crystal clear rather than telltale yellow. I looked up at the ceiling to be confronted by a long thin crack which had newly appeared. Standing on a chair, I reached up and gently touched the ceiling. It was damp. If John was here, at this point he'd have taken control. Even if he didn't know exactly what to do to solve a specific problem, he was practical enough to always figure something out.

But John was gone. I couldn't call on him to help. There was just me. I had to deal with this myself.

The loft was not and never had been my domain. It was a place I'd rarely ventured. The closest I had gotten in the past was standing on the ladder to hand stuff up to John.

The ladder creaked under my weight. I paused, not yet venturing right to the top. Even from here I could see a sliver of daylight shining through a hole in the roof.

I surveyed a mountain range made up of thirty years of accumulated stuff, preventing me from getting a closer look. Piles of boxes and a weird and wonderful assortment of objects, which at one time or another we decided were worthy of storing, stood between me and the hole in the roof.

Clearing out the loft had been one of those tasks John and I had talked about; something we always intended to get around to but never did. There was always something more fun or interesting or pressing to do instead. When we moved from our previous home, there were actually boxes we transported from one loft to the other without even opening them. The rain now coming through the hole in the roof made tackling this task a priority.

Calling on muscles not used to being used, I hauled myself up and over the top of the ladder until I was standing on a small boarded area. From here I could see the enormity of the task. Doing a 360-degree scan sent my mind into overdrive. *Where do I even start?*

Tentatively, I began to shift a few items. But it soon became clear a much more radical approach was required.

I enlisted Phoebe's help and we worked as a team. I was easily distracted by every little thing that emerged. Photographs, souvenirs, birthday cards, stuff the kids had made, their school work, old cellphones and computers, Christmas decorations, old toys. But Phoebe kept me on track.

Over the course of two days we manhandled, dropped, threw, and carried everything down that creaking ladder until the loft was completely clear. It was a precarious task. The majority of the loft was not boarded. This was the main reason John always gave for keeping me out of there. I think he probably envisioned me stepping off the rafters and disappearing though the floor, destroying the ceiling of the room below, and creating an even bigger home maintenance job for him.

'Smells like a charity shop in here.' Phoebe wrinkled her nose. Indeed, once all the items had been relocated from the loft to the house, there was a distinct *second hand* scent hanging about the place.

Looking around, I decided only things that were actually useful or had a real sentimental value would be kept. Everything else we'd send to the dump.

I looked through the array of old cards and letters the kids had made for us over the years. Flimsy aged paper covered in beautifully naïve drawings, carefully coloured in and written in childish handwriting. *Happy Birthday, Merry Christmas, Happy Mother's Day, Happy Father's Day.* They made me cry. There were cards from John to me too: *To My Girlfriend, To My Wife, Be My Valentine.* They also made me cry – every single one bringing a lump to my throat.

I wished John was here to share these precious discoveries with me. They were only meaningful to John and me. Who was I keeping them all for now?

What had started as a purely practical process became more symbolic. With every bag of rubbish I threw out, it was as if, slowly, painstakingly, bit by bit, I was letting go of what no longer served me from my old life. My body ached from the physical effort. My heart ached from the release of all the pent-up, stored emotion.

During a Zoom call with my special friend Gina, I recounted the tale about how a hole in the roof had been the catalyst for the massive clear out. I explained how I'd thrown out the junk and reorganised precious memories that were now neatly stored in plastic boxes with lids.

'Last time we spoke you said you were feeling weighed down and stuck.' She smiled at me through the computer screen. 'Maybe there was so much pent-up energy it punched a hole in the roof!'

48

THURSDAYS ONLY

THE SECOND ANNIVERSARY of John's death was looming and even though there was still no contact with Liam and Claudia, for Phoebe and I, it was important to mark the day.

We gave some thought to what we could do and where we could go. I mentioned the 1400-year-old Chapel of St Peter-on-the-wall at Bradwell-on-Sea. Although it's only a short drive from where we live, and pilgrims travel from far and wide to visit, I'd never been. It was one of those places, because of its history, John and I intended to go to but never did.

'Will it be open?' Phoebe asked.

Usually the chapel is open for people to visit anytime, but we were in the midst of Covid-19 restrictions, so I emailed to check. The reply brought a smile to my face. Due to the restrictions it was only open to the public on Thursday mornings, for a communion service.

The second anniversary of John's death, the 29th of October, 2020, was a Thursday.

Phoebe and I got up early to make sure we got there in plenty of time. Set in a field at the end of a long track, from the outside the square building looks stark. It's described as a 'place of Celtic spirituality and the oldest largely intact Christian church in England'.

We were the only people there until Reverend Steven arrived. Marching towards us, his ecclesiastical robes billowing in the breeze reminiscent of a ship's sails.

'Morning,' he beamed. 'Get yourselves a chair each.'

Phoebe and I exchanged a quizzical glance before doing as instructed. After retrieving a couple of folding chairs from the shed next to the chapel, we followed Reverend Steven inside.

So, here we were. Two years on from the day John died. Two non-religious, non-believers feeling awkward, waiting for the communion service to begin. I decided to come clean and confess to the Reverend we had no idea what to do. Kindly he explained the protocol and we told him the reason for our visit.

Sitting in that simple stone building, engaging in a religious service was not something either of us would usually do. But it felt fine. It was just us, our grief, and in a way I can't explain it was John too. Something was happening for me which I can only describe as a shift in energy.

From living almost exclusively in my head, I began to connect to my heart and my gut and to something else.

After the service, we thanked the Reverend, put the chairs back in the shed, and said our farewells. Phoebe and I walked side by side through the drizzle back along the track that led from the chapel to where we'd parked. We didn't say much. We didn't talk about the awful day John died. Nor compare this day to the first anniversary we'd shared with Liam and Claudia in Cornwall.

Pausing for a moment, I looked back across the windswept field at the chapel. Silhouetted against a sweeping palette, the green of the field, the greyish blue of the sea and the sky, I thought about the impermanence of everything. Yet that building had stood there for over a thousand years before I existed. And would likely exist long after I was gone. Without saying a word, Phoebe put her arms around me to give me the hug I didn't know I needed.

We continued, walking in the footsteps of all those who had taken that same path before us.

'Did I ever tell you about when Dad discovered his spirit animal?'

We both chuckled as I recounted the story of 'My Little Pony'.

Chapel of St Peter-on-the-wall at Bradwell-on-Sea

49

SURVIVAL

PEOPLE SAY TIME IS A HEALER. I disagree. Time alone does not heal, it merely passes. Although it is true that everything happens at its own pace. You may be desperately impatient for spring to arrive and for the tree to bud with blossom because you are tired of the bare branches of winter. But it does not happen at the time you would prefer. It happens when it happens thanks to forces from *that field* we cannot see.

There are no shortcuts out of hell. No quick fixes, either pharmacological or psychological, that will speed up the journey of grief. There is no point denying or resisting the pain because it will still be there even if you try your best to pretend it isn't. Like the dark, trying to ignore its presence does not create light.

Far from a nice neat linear journey, grief and mourning are a tripping, stumbling dance of two-steps-forward-one-step-back. Reminiscent of the traumatic flapping, flipping, gasping of a fish out of water.

In December 2020, twenty-six months after losing John, the CEO of an aptly-named charity, Next Chapter, asked me to design and deliver a pilot project. I was to offer individual coaching sessions and run a weekly psycho-education group for women with complex needs in a residential recovery refuge. The women were addicts, mostly heroin and crack. They were dealing with detox and the impact of domestic abuse. Some had been homeless and living on the street. Many had been involved in crime. Each had survived truly horrific experiences.

These women were a world away from the clients I'd seen in my private practice. In turn they could be tough, raw, loud, withdrawn, vulnerable, manipulative, aggressive, eager to please, afraid of abandonment. At first, I wasn't sure I could cut it. And John wasn't there to encourage me, to tell me that I was capable.

One by one the women began to open up to me and reveal snippets of their individual stories. I started to recognise themes. I saw parallels between them and people who would consider themselves from an entirely different world. There were similarities between their dependence on drugs, albeit illegal in their case, and what happened to John and to me. In different ways, we all sought external solutions to internal problems: prescription pills for psychological distress or illegal drugs or alcohol to numb the pain of childhood trauma and abusive relationships.

With these women it's easy to see the devastating consequences of their drug misuse. The health and social problems that accompany life as an addict are all too evident. But the drugs are not the only problem. If it was merely the substance, then everyone who ever experimented with drugs would become an addict and everyone who ever tasted alcohol would become an alcoholic.

Drug misuse is a *symptom* of something deeper: a lack of healthy tools to cope with trauma and emotional pain. Illegal drugs and even the misuse of legal substances like alcohol simply numb feelings we don't know what to do with. Just like antidepressants. They do not treat or solve the problem but rather simply mask symptoms. And bring in their wake a host of new damage.

'You know what, Denise?' a resident who had an array of mental health diagnoses said to me during a session. 'I don't think I have a mental health disorder. I think I'm just really sad about a lot of things that have happened in my life.'

This struck such a chord with me. These women are regarded by some as degenerates, social outcasts. But they're not so different from all the people, myself included, who turn to doctors to prescribe legal drugs in an attempt to numb unwanted feelings.

The way these women welcomed, engaged with, and embraced the program both humbled and inspired me. Working with these wonderful wild women changed and perhaps even saved my life. After feeling so low and worthless for so long, I began to believe that perhaps I did still have something useful to offer. Maybe my existence had meaning and purpose and I could offer these women some tools.

After one intense but rewarding day at the refuge, I returned home tired but feeling satisfied. I wandered into the living room. Running my finger along the edge of the mantel above the log burner, I noticed the dust gathering.

This is where the urn containing John's ashes sits, a pair of his glasses perched on top. I reached out to touch the cool slate of the urn. He's gone, but occasionally I do sense his presence. A feeling, a shadow glimpsed at the corner of my eye. I wish with every ounce of my being he was still here. I wish he'd never taken the pills. I wish we could go back in time to our life as it was: perfect in all its imperfections.

I looked down at the chain around my neck and the locket containing some of John's ashes and his photo. I always wear it whenever I leave the house. I wear his wedding ring too. The simple gold band with the diamond at the centre was not John's original wedding ring. He had lost that, and the second one had split as a result of the wear and tear of his physical occupation. This one he'd worn for about twenty years.

'It's amazing, you know,' John once remarked, looking at his wedding ring. 'I wear this all the time, even at work, and it survives all the knocks and punishment.' I think he would have been impressed by the fact it survived being hit by a train.

50

I AM ME BECAUSE WE WERE US
SUMMER 2021

My back aches from the effort of digging up a huge overgrown shrub. Five years ago, John and I made over the garden. He'd cleverly constructed long troughs for greenery, edging the expanse of the L-shaped deck he constructed from scratch. The plant in question had long since outgrown this space.

When John died, I lost interest in many things, including the garden, which had declined into a sad and neglected space. No longer a place of fun, laughter, and simple enjoyment. The place where John had played with squealing grandkids on the rope swing or the trampoline. The place we returned to after trips to the garden centre. Enjoying the simple pleasure of spending time selecting just the right location for each colourful purchase. No longer a place to sit in comfortable conversation deep into the night, drinking wine and tending the fire pit, cocooned in a circle of flickering fiery illumination. For a long time I simply ignored how ugly and unruly the plant had become. Along with so many other jobs that needed to be done, I'd put off dealing with it.

Until today.

In sweaty, breathless frustration I abandoned the shovel in favour of using my bare hands and brute force. With the satisfaction of victory in a tug of war, the beast conceded the battle, finally giving way. I straightened up, arching my back. My palms gritty with rich dark soil, I used the back of my hand to wipe the sweat from my forehead. It felt good to be tending the garden again.

Pleased with my progress, I decided to pause for a while before clearing up the debris of soil, roots, and leaves. Getting myself a cool apple juice I wandered to the end of the garden and took a seat in a favourite spot. The chair was strategically placed. Comfortably shaded at the hottest part of the day and bathed in the last rays of orange sun well into the evening. Sipping the sweet juice, I savoured the view.

Doug scratched at the fence, giving short loud barks in an attempt to get the attention of the dog that lived in the house on the other side. No doubt his intention was to tempt his adversary into one of their regular, rowdy, barking competitions. (These invariably erupt into a scene of mayhem, with both doing their impression of vicious guard dog, each attacking the fence from their respective side. In an attempt to halt the ensuing chaos I usually end up chasing Doug in wide sweeping circuits of the garden, while he gleefully bobs and weaves to avoid capture. With flailing arms I alternate between shouting threats and offering bribes. It's a drill I suspect he enjoys much more than I do.) Today, however, Doug's call to action goes unheeded.

Enjoying the simple pleasure of just sitting, I turn my face upwards. The warmth of the late afternoon sun feeling good on my already slightly sunburnt skin.

From somewhere not far away, the smokey fragrance of a BBQ wafts on the air. Appreciatively, I breathe in the aroma which magically transports me back to memories of big family get togethers. Slightly over-cooked sausages and blackened burgers nestling in soft fluffy white buns. Inconsequential conversations. John entertaining with his best Gordon Ramsay impression as he pokes at pieces of under cooked chicken with mock indignation.

Beautiful bird song envelopes me in surprisingly loud sweet stereo. I listen to a bee buzz past my ear. I imagine she's grateful I've returned to the garden to plant new fragrant blooms just for her.

Auntie Olive pops into my mind. She was a wonderful gardener. She grew roses with big fragrant blooms in an assortment of colours. Quite soon after they married, her husband Albert had become disabled. Although physically paralysed, his sharp mind never dimmed. Olive lovingly cared for him at home. For years she fed him, bathed him, brushed his hair and undertook all his personal care, as well as running their home and her own business. She undertook every task with a light optimism that sparkled as bright as the ever present glint in her eye. The babies she longed for were never to be. But still she made the very best of her life. She would have been as awesome as a mother as she was an aunt. I was a kind of surrogate daughter. When she died, she left life changing amounts of money as an inheritance to Jake, Phoebe, and Liam. They were the closest thing she had to grandchildren.

'Life. It's just a game, you know,' she'd often say.

My auntie, Olive Wayman, was one of the most genuinely positive people I've ever known. I try to remind myself to use the mantra she frequently repeated when facing stressful situations: *I am competent, confident, cheerful, and calm.*

During my training courses, I frequently used her as an example of sincere optimistic positivity in the face of real adversity. When some students questioned her existence, I invited her to make a guest appearance. She thoroughly enjoyed the attention and the students totally loved her.

On the day she died, aged eighty-nine, her home was immaculate. As was she. John and I were blessed to be with her when, without complaint, she drew her last breath. She left this world as she had lived in it: with grace.

Like my father, she had no time for religion or God. Denying the possibility of an afterlife, insisting it was just a made up story to give *those who needed it something to look forward to.*

Just a few days after she died, on what would have been her ninetieth birthday, I had an experience which made me wonder. A sign, perhaps, in the days before I was predisposed to notice them.

I was walking Lil, the dog we inherited from her, who loved to chase crows. I noticed a little girl who seemed very excited at seeing Lil. She pointed and pulled her parents towards us. She was only about two years old, but most insistent. After checking with me that Lil was child friendly, her obviously doting parents obliged. Delighted, she stroked and cuddled Lil who responded to this child as if greeting an old friend.

When it became apparent the little girl had no intention of moving on, her mum finally spoke up.

'Come on now, Olive, it's time to go.' My heart missed a beat.

Olive.

The memory still gives me a warm reassuring sense of something I can't quite explain. I like to imagine Olive in the afterlife she doubted saying something like, 'Well who would have thought it? Heaven does exist!' I like to think that maybe that *other field* offers her the chance to have the life with Alb she always dreamed of, including her own babies and the happily-ever-after she so deserved.

Olive's life, just like everyone else's, was not perfect. Far from it in fact. Yet she always described herself as fortunate. Focussing on what there was to be appreciative of.

Sitting in the sunshine in my garden I considered my life. Far from perfect. I am still a widow. John is still dead. For different reasons, I'm still estranged from my two sons Jake and Liam and their respective families, and from my mum. After losing John, I perhaps understood a little better why my mum changed so much after my dad died. They were married for sixty years, almost twice as long as John and I. Maybe that means her heartbreak was twice as bad as mine.

My dad once told me in no uncertain terms that I'd achieved my professional success because I had 'a good mum and a good husband.' At the time I felt hurt, like he'd underestimated how hard I worked. But actually, he was right. My mum had helped out a lot with the kids when they were little. She cooked, cleaned our house, and cared for the children enabling me to work. I miss her.

And John? Well, of course, John was never less than one hundred percent supportive of my career aspirations. I miss him.

I still have some very dark days. But I know at the level of my heart and soul that every single emotion I experience is totally within the realm of normal. On the darkest days, my thoughts and feelings are far from nice—but they are normal. Even though John is no longer here, the knowledge that *I am me because we were us* endures. I am grateful for the life we shared.

My mind drifts to thoughts of Phoebe. A brave, strong, loyal, and kind young woman. She's faced many obstacles and overcome many challenges. I am proud to be her mum. She is now living her own life to the full. Perfect? No, of course not. But a good life which I am appreciative she includes me in.

I think about Ruby and Josh, my darling grandchildren. Following the estrangement with Jake, my relationship with them continued thanks to their lovely mum, Louise. I feel immense gratitude towards her and appreciation at being part of their lives. To be included in the emergence of the next generation's unfolding story is a privilege.

Doug, seemingly bored with trying to attract the attention of the dog next door, drops a ball at my feet and barks his instruction for me to throw it.

My life is a far cry from what I'd expected, anticipated, or hoped it might be. Yet, in this moment, I feel a warmth not exclusively due to the late afternoon sun. My heart is healing and I have hope for the future. Even though I am far from certain what it might hold.

Reaching down, I give Doug's big ears a gentle scratch before throwing the ball for him.

I'm surprised to find myself thinking something, which in the immediate aftermath of John's death, I genuinely believed I would never feel again. In this moment, I am happy.

51

WEEDS AND DIRT

NOT LONG AFTER JOHN DIED, our next door neighbour, Bev, told me about an exchange she and John once had. She was in her front garden doing some weeding and spotted John over the fence washing his car.

'Why are you bothering to clean your car, it's only going to get dirty again?'

John straightened up, the sponge in his hand dripping a trail of foamy bubbles. 'Why are you digging up the weeds when they'll only grow back again?'

Even after the deepest clean, things get dirty. Even in the best maintained garden, weeds reappear.

The emotional rollercoaster of life comprises both highs and lows. As well as those long stretches in between where it just rattles along. Happiness and sadness. Elation and grief. Life whirls and spins and is glorious and excruciating and mundane all at the same time.

When struggling to cope with the various ups and downs of life, we need to remind ourselves that negative feelings are just feelings. They are not symptoms. They don't require fixing with mind-altering drugs.

The human experience is rich, deep, and complex. Life cannot be reduced to merely the biochemical. Our lives are shaped and influenced not just by what is happening physically within and to our bodies, but also by what is happening on the emotional, mental, spiritual, social, and environmental levels of existence.

Life is an ever-changing experience. Nothing is static. Nothing lasts forever. People are born, live their lives, and then die, to be replaced by new generations.

During the good times it's important to remember that nothing lasts forever in order to savour every moment. During the bad times it is important to remember that *this too shall pass*.

Life is what it is.

Weeds grow back. Cars get dirty again. The good times don't last, and neither do the bad.

Dear John

In case you ever doubted it…

I just want to say:

You were my best friend.

You were a good husband.

You were a good dad.

You were a good grandpa.

You were a good person.

Thank you for being my man for thirty-three years.

I will always be grateful to you for so, so much.

I will always love you.

I will always wish you were still here with me.

Until we meet again, in that other field…

Enjoy the ultimate ride out on your heavenly Harley.

AFTERWORD

I have learned so much more about the potential risks and side effects of certain prescription medications, and about how health systems—in particular the NHS here in the UK—tend to deal with mental health issues, than I could reasonably include in the main part of this book. But I do want to share some of that information, in the hope it might raise awareness. Perhaps it might even prevent this from happening to you or someone you love.

Even in light of what happened to John, I am not anti-medication. If you take an antidepressant and you think it helps you, keep taking it. Just remember that it is no more medicinal than a glass of wine. It may temporarily make you feel different, but it does not treat anything. Its purpose is the numbing, the blunting of the emotions. But a drug can't discern between which feelings are desirable and which are not.

"Just like other substances that affect brain chemistry (such as illicit drugs) psychiatric drugs produce altered mental states. They do not 'cure' diseases, and in many cases their mechanism of action is not properly understood."
CEP Council for Evidence Based Psychiatry

I am pro-information. And I'm against people being made to feel like they're sick, when in fact they're just thinking and feeling. Since the introduction of SSRI antidepressants we've become a society with *mental health problems* rather than simply *problems*. We've been persuaded that we're incapable of riding the waves of normal emotional response to life's challenges.

I am pro-education:

Education for prescribers and education for potential users of these drugs on the full range of side effects, especially the potentially deadly (if 'rare') side effects that cause suicidal ideation.

Education on the fact that GPs, although the main prescribers of these drugs, often have very little training in mental health and merely repeat, parrot fashion, the outdated chemical imbalance myth they have been fed by the pharmaceutical industry.

Education on the fact these drugs are psychoactive substances designed to alter the mind, and that they do not treat or cure illness.

Education that Depression and Anxiety are descriptions, not diagnosis.

Education on more holistic and healthy ways to build and maintain psychological fitness, well-being and resilience, especially during times of excessive stress and psychological distress.

Education on the dangers of over-medicalising human experience.

ON THE MYTH OF CHEMICAL IMBALANCE

"Psychiatric drugs have been prescribed to patients on the basis that they cure a 'chemical imbalance'. However, no chemical imbalances have been proven to exist in relation to any mental health disorder. There is also no method available to test for the presence or absence of these chemical imbalances.
There are no biological tests such as blood tests or brain scans that can be used to provide independent objective data in support of any psychiatric diagnosis."

Council for Evidence Based Psychiatry

ON INSOMNIA, ZOPICLONE, AND SUICIDE

"The principal new contribution of this review is the clarification regarding the timing of suicide risk related to ingestion of hypnotics. Under specific conditions, hypnotics may induce or exacerbate suicidality…"

W. Vaughn McCall, MD, MS, of Medical College of Georgia, Augusta University, Augusta

PATIENT INFORMATION FOR JOHN'S PRESCRIPTIONS.

Citalopram

Warning: Suicidal thoughts and behaviours.

Citalopram use may increase suicidal thoughts or actions in some children, teenagers, or young adults within the first few months of treatment or when the dose is changed.

Side Effects.

Symptoms such as restlessness or difficulty in sitting or standing still can also occur during the first weeks of the treatment.

Thoughts of suicide and worsening of your depression or anxiety disorder. If you are depressed and/or have anxiety disorders you can sometimes have thoughts of harming or killing yourself. These may be increased when first starting antidepressants, since these medicines all take time to work, usually about two weeks but some-times longer.

Other Medicines and Citalopram Tablets

Medicines may affect the action of other medicines and this can sometimes cause serious adverse reactions.

Side effects include:

Thoughts of harming or killing themselves.

Panic attack.

Restlessness.

Aggression.

Hallucinations.

Problems concentrating.

Loss of memory (amnesia).

Ringing in the ears (tinnitus).

Palpitations.

Tiredness.

Difficulty in sleeping.

Anxiety.

Nervousness.

Confusion.

Akathisia.

Zopiclone .

Zopiclone tablets are sleeping pills (hypnotics) which work by acting on the brain to cause sleepiness.

Side effects include:

Poor memory since taking Zopiclone (amnesia).

Seeing or hearing things that are not real (hallucinations).

Thinking things that are not true (delusions).

Feeling low or sad (depressed mood).

Feeling physically or mentally tired.

Agitation.

Feeling confused.

Feeling irritable or aggressive.

Feeling restless or angry.

Feeling lightheaded or problems with coordination.

Double vision.

Moving unsteadily or staggering.

Creeping on the skin (paraesthesia).

Difficulty paying attention.

Sleep-driving and other strange behaviour.

There have been some reports of people doing things while asleep that they do not remember when waking up after taking a sleep medicine.

This includes sleep-driving and sleepwalking.

Alcohol and some medicines for depression or anxiety can increase the chance that this serious effect will happen.

ON ANTIDEPRESSANTS AND SUICIDE

"While antidepressants are designed to decrease the symptoms of depression, they occasionally have the opposite effect and can increase suicidal thoughts, especially in children and adolescents. In 2004 the US Food and Drug Administration (FDA) issued a black box warning - the agency's strictest warning - for all selective serotonin re-uptake inhibitors (SSRI) antidepressants regarding their association with suicidal thoughts and behaviours."

Matt Mauney. 'Suicide and Antidepressants' drugwatch.com

"...can lead to suicide and violence in adults with no sign of a mental disorder.
Healthy adults who are taking certain antidepressants have a higher risk of suicidal thoughts and violent behaviour, according to the results of a systematic review.
The research suggests that selective serotonin and serotonin-

norepinephrine re-uptake inhibitors may increase the risk of events that can lead to suicide or violent behaviour in adults with no sign of a mental illness."

Debbie Andala. 'Antidepressants Associated with Increased Risk of Suicidal Thoughts in Healthy Adults'. The Pharmaceutical Journal, October 2016.

"The increased rates (of suicide) in the first twenty-eight days of starting and stopping antidepressants emphasise the need for careful monitoring of patients during this period."

Julia Hippisley-Cox et al - 'Antidepressant Use and Risk of Suicide and Attempted Suicide or Self Harm in People Aged 20 - 64.' British Medical Journal 350 2015

ON AKATHISIA AND SUICIDE IDEATION

It is my belief there was a causal link between the prescription of Zopiclone and Citalopram and John's suicide. I believe he experienced the 'rare' adverse side effects caused by these drugs. There is research indicating that Akathisia, (a state of mental agitation causing restlessness or an urgent need to move) plays a part in medication induced suicide, especially in the early days of taking such medications. Side effects can result in some people experiencing dramatic and overpowering suicide ideation.

"It is essential to treat akathisia as soon as possible. The condition can both cause a mental illness to get worse ... People may also experience suicidal thoughts because of akathisia."

Jenna Fletcher, 'What is Akathisia and why does it occur?'
Medical News Today

The authors of a research study in Australia examined more than 120 people who had been diagnosed with Akathisia / Serotonin Toxicity after taking prescribed medication designed to treat psychosocial distress. Eight of those 120 had committed homicide and many had become violent while taking antidepressants.

"The results ...presented here concerning a sample of persons given antidepressants for psychosocial distress demonstrate the extent to which the psychopharmacology industry has expanded its influence beyond its ability to cure."

Y.Lucire and C. Crotty, Pharmacogenomics and personalised medicine, 2011

ON THE GROWING USE OF ANTIDEPRESSANTS

"Around thirteen per cent of Americans take antidepressants, and their use is growing around the world. In the UK, the prescription of antidepressants has doubled over the past ten years. The long term use of the drugs is also increasing, year on year. In 2000, around 5 million Americans had been taking antidepressants for five years or more. By 2018, this had increased to 15.5 million. At the same point, almost 25 million adults had been taking antidepressants for more than two years, a sixty per cent increase from 2010."

Steven Taylor, PhD, 'An Epidemic of Antidepressants, Why We Need Non-chemical Treatments for Depression.' Psychology Today

"Negative effects (of prescribed antidepressant drugs) are often misdiagnosed. Psychiatric drugs can have effects that include mental disturbance, suicide, violence, and withdrawal syndromes.

They can be misdiagnosed as new psychiatric presentations, for which additional drugs may be prescribed, sometimes leading to long-term use of multiple different psychiatric drugs in the same person."

Council For Evidence Based Psychiatry.

ON ANTIDEPRESSANTS AS THE ONLY TREATMENT FOR DEPRESSION

Dr Michael Yapko, an American psychologist and expert on depression, expresses concern that people take medication without being offered therapy alongside.

"It's not enough, and here's why it's not enough. No amount of medication is going to help you develop skills in managing stress. None. No amount of medication's going to help you develop a better attribution or explanatory style or help you build and maintain positive relationships with other people or help you develop the kinds of cognitive skills that help you think critically about experiences instead of just getting sucked in by your feelings. It's not going to help you develop problem solving skills. It's not going to help you develop better decision making strategies. It's not going to teach you how to build a support network with people. It's not going to help you come to terms with whatever crummy things have happened in your life, and it's certainly not going to help you build ... one of the most important

things, one of the most important things in getting treatment is how to build a compelling future."

Dr Michael Yapko, 'How to prevent depression'
psychlopaedia.org, Australian Psychological Association.

In my personal experience as a patient, from what I know about John's experience, and from what I have been told by others, SSRIs are often the only treatment offered. This appears to go against the National Institute for Clinical Excellence (NICE) guidelines. For people with mild to moderate depressive symptoms, NICE guidelines do not suggest drugs as the first intervention.

"Do not use antidepressants routinely to treat persistent sub threshold depressive symptoms or mild depressive symptoms because the risk/benefit ratio is poor."

The NICE guidelines also state that:

"Patients and, where appropriate families and carers should be provided with information on the nature, course and treatment of depression including the use and likely side-effect profile of medication."

In my opinion it is not sufficient to merely include a leaflet in the packaging. Alerting patients and their next of kin to be vigilant about side effects could save lives. Much is said about suicide prevention - this is a simple way to prevent avoidable deaths.

The NICE guidelines also state that:

"When prescribing SSRIs, healthcare professionals should actively seek out signs of akathisia, suicidal ideation, and increased anxiety and agitation. They should also advise patients of the risk of these symptoms in the early stages of treatment and advise them to seek help promptly if these are at all distressing."

In my own personal experience of GPs prescribing SSRI's for my 'depression', and in everything I learned about the information provided to John and others I've spoken with, this does not happen. In fact GPs are likely to say something along the lines of the drugs 'do not work for the first couple of weeks'. Making people believe that it is their 'mental health issues', rather than the side effects of the drugs that are making them feel worse. If GPs are not fully informed, how can they advise patients? If patients are not told about the dangers of potential side effects, people will continue to suffer and even die unnecessarily.

ON GP'S AND MENTAL HEALTH TRAINING

There are many excellent GPs and I do not believe that anyone would become a doctor unless they had a desire to help people. However, GP's are not specialists. If you had a heart attack you would want to be treated by a cardiologist. If you required brain surgery you would reasonably expect to be referred to a neurosurgeon. So, why when it comes to mental health are GPs routinely expected to act like specialists?

There isn't even mandatory practise-based training in mental health for GP's, even though more than forty percent of all GP appointments in the UK involve mental health issues. And that percentage is rising.

Fewer than half GP trainees complete any kind of mental health training placements.

More than eighty percent of people prescribed drugs for mental health issues – including me and John – are treated by a GP.

ON MENTAL HEALTH VERSUS MENTAL ILLNESS

Since the introduction of SSRIs, mental illness has been kind of re-branded as mental health. Even though, in reality, mental health is so much more than the mere absence of illness. Much of the funding for mental health campaigns which encourage people to seek help from their GP's, originates from the very companies who profit from the sales of antidepressant drugs. Arguably making these campaigns more about marketing drugs than focussed on improving public health.

'It's okay not to be okay. Talk to your doctor. You have a chemical imbalance. Take these pills. They are will make you mentally healthy!'

As a result of these campaigns more and more people who are feeling unhappy or anxious – for whatever reason – self-diagnose with mental health issues and contact a GP who more than likely will prescribe antidepressants. Feelings have become regarded as a fault to be fixed, a condition requiring treatment, rather than in many cases a normal if not nice response to adverse life experiences and challenging circumstances.

JOHN'S CASE IS NOT ISOLATED

If John's case was an isolated one, you could dismiss me as a delusional grieving widow in denial. But there are others. Lots of others. I've received many messages - here are a few - I've changed the names for privacy purposes.

"My sister took her own life on the railway on 31st August. I have completed my statement for the inquest but I worry the coroner will just rubber stamp this as mental health. But it wasn't. My sister had never had any mental health issues. It all happened this year and within five months she had stepped in front of a train." - Rosalie

"My husband killed himself on 26th October 2019, ten days after he was prescribed antidepressants for anxiety and to help him sleep. He had never suffered depression in his life." - Cathy

"My father tragically took his own life after a very short and rapid period of anxiety and depression. I recall researching not long after his death, and finding that the medication he was on could increase the risk of suicide. We were unaware and uninformed at the time, and despite the warnings his dosage had just been increased." - Mary

ON CORONER'S CONCLUSIONS AND SUICIDE

"The lowering of the standard of proof, from criminal to civil, means that coroners and jurors may return a verdict of suicide on 'the balance of probabilities'. This is likely to mean that more deaths will be classified as suicides in future. This is something that Samaritans and others have been calling for, for several years because we believe it will help get a more accurate picture of the number of people who take their own lives and help to reduce the stigma around suicide."

Samaritans Suicide Statistics Report, December 2018

I believe there are problems inherent in the archaic inquest system, resulting in inconsistencies in verdicts/conclusions. Following the inquest into John's death, I noticed several discrepancies in conclusions/verdicts given by different coroners within Essex. Even after the lowering of the standard of proof for suicide described above. I wrote to Caroline Beasley - Murray, who at the time was still senior coroner for Essex, requesting information on the objective criteria used in deciding specific conclusions/verdicts. This request was ignored.

ON WHY THE PART PLAYED BY ANTIDEPRESSANTS IN SUICIDE IS FREQUENTLY OVERLOOKED

Overwhelmed and under informed GP's who are too quick to issue prescriptions for antidepressant drugs, are part of the problem.

Pharmaceutical companies with products to sell are part of the problem.

Political systems that prefer not to address issues of inequality, poor education, poverty and social deprivation - and instead find the explanation that people *feel depressed or anxious,* due to problems with their individual mental health, are part of the problem.

The prevalence of 'toxic positivity' - the idea by that unless we are totally happy and fulfilled all the time we are suffering from poor mental health, is part of the problem.

People with problems have been transformed into patients needing prescriptions. We have been seduced into believing there is a medical solution - a quick pill shaped fix for the psychological impact of life's stress and distress.

Whenever someone who is taking drugs prescribed because they have 'a mental health issue' takes their own life, side effects are rarely considered. Instead it is accepted that the reason the person died, is because of their poor mental health. After all, that is why they were prescribed drugs! A person is deemed to be depressed because they are prescribed antidepressants. These drugs are known to make people, who were not previously, suicidal. This 'rare' side effect is not disputed. Even so, if someone kills themselves after taking these drugs - their 'mental health problem' is frequently regarded as the *only* explanation.

This means deaths are not reported as being the possible result of side effects, ensuring the side effect remains so 'rare' as not to have to be considered! A very neat circular logic prevails ensuring there is no need to investigate further.

BOOKS

Davies, James. *Cracked: Why Psychiatry is Doing More Harm Than Good.* London, UK. Icon Books, 2014. A MUST READ FOR ANYONE WHO HAS THE SLIGHTEST INTEREST IN THE MEDICALISATION OF HUMAN EMOTION. This book helped me realise I wasn't going mad!

Blackford Newman, Katinka. *The Pill That Steals Lives: One Woman's Terrifying Journey to Discover the Truth About Antidepressants.* London, UK. John Blake Publishing Ltd., 2016.

Kirsh, Irving. *The Emperor's New Drugs: Exploding the Antidepressant Myth.* New York, NY, USA. Basic Books (Hachette), reprinted 2011.

Timimi, Sami. *Insane Medicine: How the Mental Health Industry Creates Damaging Treatment Traps and How you can Escape Them.* Independently published, 2021.

Moncrieff, Joanna. *A Straight Talking Introduction to Psychiatric Drugs: The Truth About How They Work and How to Come Off Them.* Monmouth, UK. PCCS Books, 2nd Edition, 2020.

Kinderman, Peter. *A Prescription for Psychiatry: Why We Need a Whole New Approach to Mental Health and Wellbeing.* Hampshire, UK. Palgrave Macmillan, 2014.

Watson, Jo. *Drop the Disorder! Challenging the Culture of Psychiatric Diagnosis.* Monmouth, UK. PCCS Books, 2019.

WEBSITES

Council for Evidence-Based Psychiatry

'CEP exists to communicate evidence of the potentially harmful effects of psychiatric drugs to the people and institutions in the UK that can make a difference.'

cepuk.org

AntiDepAware

'Promoting awareness of the dangers of antidepressants.'

antidepaware.co.uk

Antidepressant Risks

'Helping people understand the risks of taking antidepressants.'

antidepressantrisks.org

ACKNOWLEDGMENTS

To John, my partner in crime and best friend, for everything, always, obviously.

To Phoebe, my amazing daughter, for literally being my reason to stay alive and for continuing your dad's legacy of laughter. (Did you hear me call?!)

To Liam and Claudia for the love and support.

To Jacob for being my first born.

To all the friends who checked up on me, who thought of ways to make me smile, who cared… including:

June C. for all your help with the inquest stuff.

Cath C. for all the coffee and cake.

Nicky C. for having a cheque book and coming with me to get the recording.

Karl G. for the wine, chocolate, flowers, home baked scones, and for being handy with a chainsaw and a hammer.

Alistair and Kirsten S. for being there.

Andy H. for being John's friend and then mine.

Chris and Joy F. for always making me feel so welcome.

Gina M. for letting me cry and reminding me I'm not responsible for bringing anyone else down. And for describing me as your friend 'the writer'!

Thank you to all the brave souls – including **Colleen B** – and **Brian**, who speak their truth about the dangerous side effects of antidepressants. In doing so you prove John's is not an isolated case.

Thank you to anyone else I may not have referred to by name. If I've ever told you I love you or I've thanked you for being in my life, I acknowledge you!

Thank you to my four-legged furry family for making me get up out of bed, eventually.

Chloe   Olivia

Lil   Doug

Happier times John, Liam, Denise & Phoebe

Denise was a psychological therapist, coach, and trainer who shared her life with John, her husband and best friend, for thirty-three years until his suicide in 2018.

Denise is now mostly trying to decide what she wants to be when she grows up.

To find out more about Denise and keep up to date with future books and projects, you can visit:

www.denise-collins.com

You can also email Denise on: hello@denise-collins.com

Printed in Great Britain
by Amazon

79222331R00192